Dutch Pictures from the Royal Collection

Dutch Pictures
from the Royal Collection

The Queen's Gallery
Buckingham Palace   *1971-72*

Designed by Graham Johnson/Lund Humphries
Printed by Lund Humphries, London and Bradford

27,30 Melchior de Hondecoeter

Jonkheer Frederik van Kretschmar of
the Stichting Iconographisch Bureau
and Jonkheer Henri van der Wyck of the
Rijksdienst voor de Monumentenzorg in
The Hague have identified the house
in the background of these two pictures
as Nijenrode Castle on the river Vecht
north of Utrecht.

The castle had been badly damaged
by the French in 1672. It was sold
to a prosperous Amsterdam merchant,
Johan Ortt (1642-1701), who became
Lord of the Manor in 1675 and completely
restored the Castle. He loved country
pursuits, built a riding-school and
stables for at least fifty horses and
was the owner of a famous stud of riding
and carriage horses. The architectural
elevation seen in No.30 apparently
survives almost unchanged. Jonkheer
van Kretschmar is inclined to believe
that the figures in these pictures
were painted by Hondecoeter's nephew
and collaborator, Jan Weenix.

37 Possible

22 May try

Notes on the furnishings.

DUTCH PICTURES.

In the eighteenth century in France collectors of seventeenth century Dutch paintings displayed their paintings in rooms furnished with contemporary French furniture, porcelain and bronzes. George IV likewise combined Dutch paintings with French eighteenth century works of art in his rooms at Carlton House. The furniture and ornaments which have been selected for this exhibition are all French. Though the furnishings are much sparser than they would have been in Carlton House, they do give some idea of the effect which must have been achieved by this combination.

LOCATION.
(Nos. denote
exhibit nos.)

In the corner. Arm-chair (late eighteenth century).
Under 4.
Of beechwood, carved and gilded and upholstered in modern green velvet.

Stamped by Georges Jacob (Master 1765-1814). It forms part of a set bought by the French dealer Dominique Daguerre, whom George IV employed to furnish Carlton House in the late 1780s and early 1790s. These particular arm-chairs were intended for the Drawing Room.

Under 5. Cabinet (last quarter of the eighteenth century).
Of oak veneered with ebony and inlaid with nineteen plaques of pietra dura. The mounts are of gilt bronze.

Stamped by M. Carlin (Master 1766-85), it was bought by George IV, probably in the late 1820s. The pietre dure panels were originally made for a Louis XIV piece of furniture by the Florentine artist G-A. Giachetti, who was employed at the Gobelins Manufactory in Paris.

In the corners. Pair of candle-stands (early eighteenth century).
Of oak veneered with a design of brass and pewter, on a ground of tortoise-shell. The mounts are of gilt bronze. The underside of the circular top is also veneered, but in this case with a design in tortoise-shell on a ground of brass.

Under 13. Marble-topped table (last quarter of the eighteenth century).
Of oak veneered with ebony and inlaid with four panels of pietra dura and plaques of jasper. The gilt bronze mounts include two female caryatid figures. The slab is of red granite.

Stamped by A. Weisweiler (Master 1778), the table was bought by George IV on 9th November in 1816 for 7,250 francs from the Parisian dealer Rocheux.

Under 22. Cabinet (late eighteenth century).
Of oak veneered with ebony and inset with five lacquer panels. The mounts are of gilt bronze and the slab is of grey-blue marble.

Under 22 cont.	Stamped by Joseph Baumhauer (Master before 1767-1772). Bought by George IV in 1825 together with a pair of matching corner-cupboards. The three pieces formerly belonged to the duchesse de Mazarin, and can be identified in the catalogue of her sale held in Paris (10-15 December 1781, Lots 218-219). The two flanking lacquer panels on the front represent a cock fight and originally formed a single panel. The centre panel, which is European, was probably inserted by Joseph.

Lacquer bowl and cover (eighteenth century).

Of early eighteenth century Japanese lacquer. The bowl is fitted with mid-eighteenth century French gilt bronze mounts. Like the table under No.13, George IV bought this bowl from the dealer Rocheux in 1816 at a cost of 400 francs.

Under 29.

Cabinet (late eighteenth century).

Of oak veneered with ebony, brass and tortoise-shell, and inlaid with six panels of pietra dura. The mounts are gilt bronze and the slab is of brocatelle marble.

Stamped by A. Weisweiler (Master 1778), the cabinet was acquired by George IV sometime before 1807.

Lacquer vase (eighteenth century).

Of early eighteenth century Japanese lacquer, the bowl is fitted with French gilt bronze mounts dating from the middle of the eighteenth century. This vase and its companion were bought by George IV and were formerly in his Library at Brighton Pavilion.

Under 33.

Arm-chair (late eighteenth century).

Of beechwood, carved and gilded and upholstered in modern green velvet.

Stamped by Georges Jacob (Master 1765-1814). It forms part of a set bought by the French dealer Dominique Daguerre, whom George IV employed to furnish Carlton House in the late 1780s and early 1790s. These particular arm-chairs were intended for the Drawing Room.

Under 35.

Cabinet (late eighteenth century).

Of oak veneered with mahogany and enriched with gilt bronze mounts.

The cabinet is not stamped, but is in the manner of A. Weisweiler or B. Molitor.

Lacquer vase (eighteenth century).

Of eighteenth century Japanese lacquer, the bowl is fitted with French gilt bronze mounts dating from about 1780.

Contents

Introduction

Queen Elizabeth I, with her instinctive devotion to the ideal of a sovereign's authority and her loathing of rebellion, could never bring herself to like the Dutch. She was accustomed to treating with fellow-sovereigns and could not talk on equal terms with 'Sovereign Lords Millers and Cheesemen' or 'Swag-bellied Dutch butter-boxes', rebels and heretics who had thrown off the yoke of their natural lord and were creating across the North Sea an urban, commercial, middle-class and anti-dynastic state. Not until 1585 did she commit herself, by the Treaty of Nonsuch, to the support of the rebel provinces by maintaining a military force in the Netherlands: a force which became a nursery for English professional soldiers. Earlier, after the States of Holland had abjured the authority of Spain, a mission from the Prince of Orange had offered to the Queen the Sovereignty of the Netherlands as 'Lady and Countess of Holland and Zeeland'. A portrait of the Prince hung at Whitehall, near the portraits of the King of Spain and the earlier likenesses of the Burgundian rulers of the Netherlands. During the Queen's reign a host of refugees from the Low Countries, seeking shelter from war and savage religious persecution, settled in England. The craftsmen and artists among them were to enrich the cultural life of their adopted country. The Hoefnagel, Hondius, Gheeradts, De Critz and Droeshout families, for example, among the many who 'came over for religion', had considerable influence on the development of the arts in this country. The lives of these exiled families and of their descendants revolved round the Dutch Reformed Church in Austin Friars. Perhaps the most important contact made on behalf of the Queen herself with a Dutch painter was the payment to Cornelis Ketel of Gouda, who was in England from 1573 to 1581, of £5 13s. 4d. for his picture for the Queen of one of the 'strange men' captured by Frobisher on his voyages to discover the North-West Passage.[1]

---

[1] W. B. Rye, *England as seen by Foreigners* (1865), pp.205–6; L. Cust, 'Foreign Artists of the Reformed Religion working in London', *Huguenot Society*, vol. VII (1903), pp.1–38; for a recent discussion of Elizabeth I's attitude towards the Netherlands, see C. Wilson, *Queen Elizabeth and the Revolt of the Netherlands* (1970).

James I disliked rebels no less heartily than his predecessor had done. Nevertheless, during his reign artistic and cultural ties were strengthened between England and the United Provinces, where a unique state was being created on the basis of military victories, political stabilization and an astonishing growth in economic prosperity. In the fields of literature, education and theological argument these links had developed in the Tudor period. James's consort, Anne of Denmark, was said by the 1st Earl of Salisbury to prefer her pictures to living people.[2] Among her pictures at Somerset House at the time of her death in 1617 were pictures of 'Dutch Kitchens', with bread, cheese and bacon or with a dead hare; a 'Dutch Boare'; and a portrait of Sir Ralph Winwood who had been the King's representative to the States-General.[3] During the reign of James I official relations between England and the United Provinces deteriorated steadily as the two countries became involved in maritime and mercantile rivalry. In the spring of 1610 an embassy from the States-General, the first of its kind to be sent out to England from the new republic, came to London, partly to induce the King to annul a decree which demanded the payment of dues for the right to fish off the British coast. The States-General were anxious to gain the friendship of the King's elder son Henry, Prince of Wales. They were told that the Prince would be pleased to accept 'some fine paintings by the best masters' in Holland and they brought over for him an exciting picture of the Battle off Gibraltar and a painting of a storm at sea; the first was by Hendrick Vroom, the second may have been by Porcellis.[4] The pictures were placed in the gallery which Inigo Jones had designed for the Prince.[5] In 1611 negotiations were set on foot, through Sir Edward Conway, for a visit to London by Michiel van Miereveld of Delft, who was regarded at that time as 'the most excellent Painter of all the Low-Countries' and whom the Prince was apparently

---

[2] *Calendar of State Papers, Domestic,* vol. IX, p.96.

[3] The inventory is preserved at the Duchy of Cornwall Office.

[4] J. G. van Gelder, 'The "Dutch Gift" of 1610 . . .', *Burlington Magazine,* vol. CV (1963), pp.541–4.

[5] They were seen there in 1613 by the Duke of Saxe-Weimar (W. B. Rye, op. cit., pp.159–67).

prepared to attach to his service.[6] Miereveld did not come, although in July he was said to be ready to embark for England; but the Prince owned at least one picture by him (No.93; Plate 36) and possibly his portrait of Sir Edward Cecil which was recorded in the time of Charles I at Hampton Court.[7]

At Prince Henry's untimely death in 1612, his collections passed to his younger brother Charles. He too disliked the Dutch and was involved, after his accession in 1625, in ludicrous attempts to establish British dominion over the surrounding seas; but, as the most discerning patron and collector who has ever graced the British throne, he was constantly looking out for artists and craftsmen who could be attracted from the Continent to his service and was as anxious to collect works by living painters as he was to swell his celebrated collection of Renaissance works of art: a collection which was looked after, incidentally, by three Dutchmen, Abraham van der Doort, Jan van Belcamp and Daniel Soreau. In March 1636 a special embassy was again sent by the States-General to London in an effort to improve relations between the two countries. The embassy brought presents to the court, including five pictures, which had probably all belonged to the Knights of St John at Haarlem. Among them was a *St Jerome*, attributed to Lucas van Leyden, and the two celebrated panels, now in Vienna, by Geertgen tot Sint Jans.[8]

Ambassadors and special envoys from the English court could play a special part in looking out for pictures for the King or in making contacts with foreign painters as Conway and Sir Edward Cecil had done in the case of Miereveld. Sir Dudley Carleton, for example, Ambassador to The Hague from 1616 to

---

[6] T. Birch, *The Life of Henry Prince of Wales* (1760), pp.479–99. Privy Purse payments on behalf of the Prince included payments (16 May 1610) 'to the Estates of Hollands men with divers pictures to his highnes'; a payment of £60 (28 June 1610) to 'the Dutch [Youth?] whom the Prince of Holland recomended to his highnes'; £2 paid to Sir Edward Cecil (9 July 1610) for a cast 'broght out of Holland'; and two payments of £20 (18 December 1609 and 29 March 1610) 'to Cornelius the Dutchman at his Highnes command' (P.R.O., S.P.14/57, 87).

[7] The portrait has not been identified.

[8] J. Bruyn and O. Millar, 'The "Dutch Gift" to Charles I', *Burlington Magazine*, vol. CIV (1962), pp.291–4. The *St Jerome* is probably the picture, now attributed to Aertgen van Leyden, in the Rijksmuseum (1433, H.1); the King bought from Sir James Palmer three panels (now at Hampton Court) which may also be by Aertgen.

1625, was in contact with Miereveld within a few months of taking up this post and sat twice to him for his portrait. In the autumn of 1616 he went on a 'pettie progresse' to Haarlem, Leiden, Amsterdam and Utrecht, the principal centres of artistic activity in the United Provinces. At Haarlem he visited Cornelis Cornelisz., Vroom and Goltzius. In June 1621 he wrote from The Hague about 'a young man growing into reputacōn in these parts who began wth Bloomer of Utrecht (where he dwells likewise) & hath bene for some yeares at Rome & other parts of Italy to mend his art: wch consisting much in night works . . .'[9] The 'young man' who had been a pupil of Bloemaert was Gerrit van Honthorst, who visited London in the spring of 1628. He stayed here until December, working principally for the King and the Duke of Buckingham. The Duke, a lavish collector of pictures with a special liking for painters of the Utrecht school, sat to Honthorst with his family for the group (No.29; Plate 2) which the King placed in his Bedchamber at Whitehall 'In a Carved guilded frame'. The Duke plays the part of Mercury in the huge masque-like allegory at Hampton Court in which the King and Queen appear as Apollo and Diana receiving the homage of the Liberal Arts; in 1681 the picture was actually described as 'a Mask wherein the King and Queen, the Duke of Buckingham and his Duchess, and many ladies are done to the life'. In the following year Honthorst painted for the King another large allegory, this time of his sister, the Queen of Bohemia, with her husband as Seladon and Astrea: 'The King and Queene of Bohemia and their Childeren in manner of Storie' which the King hung in the gallery at St James's.[10]

Other Dutch painters visited the court of Charles I. In the late 1630's Cornelis van Poelenburgh and the Fleming Alexander Keirincx were living in houses in Orchard Street which had been taken for them by the King; Jan Lievens seems to have been in England in the same decade and to have painted a portrait of the King; Ter Borch was in London in the summer of 1635. Hen-

---

[9] W. N. Sainsbury, *Original Unpublished Papers . . .* (1859), pp.13–14, 290–1.

[10] *The Journal of James Yonge;* ed. F. N. L. Poynter (1963), p.172. *Seladon and Astrea* is now in the collection of S.K.H. Prince Ernst August of Hanover. Honthorst painted a single portrait of Charles I (now in the National Portrait Gallery (4444)); the King owned a portrait by Honthorst of Henrietta Maria as a shepherdess.

drick Vroom of Haarlem had been in London in the 1620's, when he had painted, among other seapieces, a large view of the fleet bringing Prince Charles back from Spain in 1623 and had designed the famous set of tapestries of the Defeat of the Spanish Armada to hang in the House of Lords. Adam Willaerts came to England and painted, probably some years after the event, views of the fleet (e.g., No.86; Plate 4) which escorted the Elector Palatine and his bride across to Flushing in 1613. They show a development in marine painting towards a richer, more naturalistic, mood than Vroom's involved mannerist style. Within the royal collection such pictures should perhaps be seen in the same tradition as the crowded pageant-pieces of Henry VIII's journey to meet Francis I in 1520.

The little group of Charles I and his family (No.61; Plate 3), painted by Pot in 1632, and Honthorst's *Apollo and Diana*, illustrate the King's desire to have in his service painters from abroad of the highest class who could proclaim in their designs the splendours of the British sovereign and the Stuart dynasty. The formal stagecraft in Pot's little design and Honthorst's big allegories is used to present themes which were to be handled with more virtuosity and in a subtler language by the two great painters whom Charles I was to attract from the Southern, or Spanish, Netherlands: Rubens and Van Dyck. As early as 1618 Charles I, while he was still Prince of Wales, had probably sat to Daniel Mytens of Delft. He seems to have attached Mytens to his service before his accession in 1625, when he became 'one of our picture drawers of our chamber in ordinary'. Mytens, perhaps the most distinguished Dutch court portrait-painter of the age, produced the official portraits of the King before the arrival of Van Dyck in 1632. His English portraits have a sober grandeur which can sometimes remind one of early Velázquez. After Mytens's departure the King kept his *Self-portrait* (No.6; Plate 38), in its 'black Ebbone frame', hanging next to self-portraits by Rubens and Van Dyck in a little room at Whitehall. The King and members of the Whitehall circle of collectors were beginning to be fascinated by the ingenious detail in the work of living Dutch painters. Carleton, for example, had given to the King an oval *Still Life* by Jan Torrentius of 'Two rennish wine glasses . . . wherein the reflexion of the steeple of Herlam is observed', and a picture by him of a naked figure with a money-bag, a looking-glass, a skull, a book, a spider and two arrows 'whereof the invention and meaning is unknowne'.[11] In 1630 the King had actually written to the Prince of Orange, begging him to release the painter from prison in Haarlem and send him to England where he would be employed *en l'exercise de c'est Art*. Torrentius was released and in December was on his way to London, bearing some pictures 'to shew for samplers of what hee is able to doe': including the unexplained allegorical piece and an allegory of Temperance which was also taken over by the King.[12] It was probably through an envoy such as Carleton that Charles I acquired his Ter Brugghen (No.1; Plate 1): one of the drunken, laughing fellows of a type often painted by Ter Brugghen to please patrons in Utrecht and conceived under the influence of Honthorst and Baburen. The Ter Brugghen was owned during the Interregnum by Lely; and Ter Brugghen's influence can be discerned in Lely's early work, notably in his beautiful series of *Musicians.* On the other hand, Pot's *Startling Introduction,* delicately painted and elusive in subject, may have been painted for the King while Pot was in London. The inventories of the King's collection also include the names of Scorel, Heemskerck, Goltzius, Vollenhoven, Breenbergh, Houckgeest, Moreelse, De Heem, Van Nieulandt and, possibly, Van Goyen.

Relations between the Stuarts and the house of Orange had their influence on the artistic ties between the two countries. Prince Frederick Henry attached importance to marriages which would strengthen the position of his dynasty and give it a truly royal lustre. When negotiations were under way for the marriage between the King's eldest daughter, Mary, and Prince William of Orange, Prince Frederick Henry's heir, portraits of the young Prince and his parents were sent over to the King;[13] a portrait of the Princess by Van Dyck was sent over in exchange. The little pair were painted together in their wedding costumes by Van Dyck. Honthorst's large double portraits, from a slightly

---

[11] 'Abraham van der Doort's Catalogue', ed. O. Millar, *Walpole Society,* vol. xxxvii (1960), pp.64, 69.

[12] W. H. Carpenter, *Pictorial Notices . . .* (1844), pp.192–4; W. N. Sainsbury, op. cit., pp.347–9. The allegory of Temperance, signed and dated 1614, is in the Rijksmuseum (2311 d).

[13] The portrait of the young Prince, with that of his father by Honthorst, is at Windsor.

1 Detail from Plate 2

11 Detail from Plate 5

III Detail from Plate 5

IV Detail from Plate 14

later date, of the young couple and the Prince's parents, and the large dynastic pictures painted by Honthorst for the Oranjezaal in the Huis ten Bosch, are the closest approach made by a Dutch painter to the more accomplished glorifications designed by Van Dyck and Rubens for Stuarts, Medici, Bourbons or Habsburgs. They represent an attempt by the Orange family to establish in Holland a courtly, international baroque style which was essentially alien to the Dutch spirit. In the 1630's Honthorst had been employed continuously to paint portraits of the Queen of Bohemia and her family, some of which were destined for Charles I. In 1629 her eldest son, Frederick Henry, whose portrait by David Baudringhien hung in the Bear Gallery at Whitehall, was drowned in the Zuider Zee. A mission of condolence set off under the leadership of Sir Robert Kerr. While he was in Holland Sir Robert met Constantine Huygens, Secretary to the Prince of Orange. Huygens's long career covers many aspects of the cultural relationship between England and Holland. At the time of Kerr's visit Huygens was beginning an autobiography in Latin which included a discussion of the state of painting in the Netherlands and of a number of living painters, including Rembrandt and his associate in Leiden, Jan Lievens: young men of humble origins, whom Huygens put in the highest class and for whom he prophesied a famous future. A mutual admiration for the poems of John Donne was a bond between Kerr and Huygens. Kerr returned from his mission with three pictures for the King which had probably been handed to him by the Prince of Orange and could have been procured by Huygens: a painting of 'a young Scholler Sitting uppon a Stoole . . . reading in a booke by a Seacole fire', stated to be by Rembrandt, but probably by Lievens; a *Self-portrait* by Rembrandt;[14] and the 'old woman with a greate Scarfe upon her heade' by Rembrandt (No.4; Plate 6). All three were placed in the Long Gallery towards the Orchard at Whitehall: the two portraits in black frames and the *Self-portrait* placed 'above my Lo: Ankroms doore'.[15] Kerr's return to London, with pictures which would have given the court its first sight of Rembrandt, is a momentous occasion in the history of English

---

[14] Almost certainly the *Self-portrait* in the Walker Art Gallery, Liverpool.

[15] 'Abraham van der Doort's Catalogue', op. cit., pp.57, 60; C. White, 'Did Rembrandt ever visit England?', *Apollo*, vol. LXXVI (1962), pp.177–84.

taste. In our eyes they would have seemed the outstanding items in the first important collection of Dutch pictures to be built up outside the Low Countries.

On 23 May 1660 Charles II and his brothers set sail from the beach at Scheveningen on their triumphal voyage to England. The exiles' first taste of the pleasures of the promised land came when they were lavishly entertained, with their aunt, the Queen of Bohemia, their sister, the Princess of Orange, and their small nephew, the Prince of Orange, in The Hague by the States-General on the eve of the Restoration. During the new King's reign the commercial and maritime rivalry between the two countries became so intense that they twice led to open naval warfare in the 1660's and 1670's. But cultural links between them continued to thrive. During their exile the King and many of his supporters had been painted by Dutch artists. The aged Sir Robert Kerr, now Earl of Ancram, had sat to Lievens in Amsterdam in 1652. Cornelius Johnson, Honthorst, Pieter Nason, Hanneman and Simon Luttichuys painted the royal brothers and their needy followers. Honthorst painted the Duke of Monmouth's mother, a portrait which was at Whitehall – in store – after the Restoration. Hanneman seems to have been particularly popular with the exiles. His earliest portraits (e.g., No.3; Plate 35) show something of a Venetian romance fused with his inborn Dutch reserve; the sitters may have come from the families of the refugee artists and craftsmen. Hanneman quickly absorbed the Van Dyck manner. The exaggerated fluency of his handling and his stagey designs probably endeared him to sitters to whom the name of Van Dyck would have conjured up memories of happier days. It was natural that he should have been commissioned by Prince Frederick Henry's widow to paint portraits (e.g., No.8; Plate 70) of the little Prince of Orange for his other grandmother, Henrietta Maria, and his aunt, the Duchess of York. The portraits were sent to England in June 1664 and were a great success. In November 1660 Charles II received, as his father and uncle had done, a present, including a fine group of pictures, from the States of Holland. The States had selected twenty-four pictures from the Reynst collection and added to them three pictures bought from Gerrit Dou. They included his *Young Mother,* which the King particularly admired. It had been painted two years earlier.

Dou, who had joined Rembrandt, as his first pupil, in 1628, at the time when Huygens was writing about the young geniuses of Leiden, achieved early success. He founded the Leiden school of *Feinmalerei,* painting small pictures in minute detail and with flawless craftsmanship: a style which remained popular with collectors until the nineteenth century. Charles II is said to have invited Dou to London: an invitation which Dou evaded because he felt that the life of a court painter would be uncongenial. The 'Dutch Gift' also included a superb Saenredam, painted in 1648, of the interior of the Church of S. Bavo in Haarlem. This is by far the earliest reference to a picture by this great artist being in a collection outside Holland; and it seems that the royal collection was still, as it had been before the Civil War, the most important collection of Dutch pictures outside Holland.[16] The Dou and the Saenredam later, sadly, left the royal collection. In 1660 and 1662 the King bought a group of pictures from William Frizell which included the two pictures by Maerten van Heemskerck which are still at Hampton Court (e.g., No.94; Plate 33) and a *Deluge*, by the same painter, which is apparently lost. The Dutch art-dealer, Gerrit Uylenburgh, who had helped to put the 'Dutch Gift' together for the States, was later employed by Charles II as 'Picture-Keeper'. He was succeeded by another Dutchman, Frederick Sonnius. Pieter van der Faes, who had been trained in Haarlem, had come to England, where he is invariably known as Peter Lely, in the 1640's. In October 1661 he was appointed Principal Painter to Charles II. His strong and sensuous style captures the mood of the Restoration court, but his portrait of Princess Mary (No.16; Plate 71) has an unexpected freshness.

A fundamental change in English foreign policy, in face of the growing menace of Louis XIV's ambitions, was symbolized by the marriage on 4 November 1677 of the Princess and her cousin, the Prince of Orange, Stadtholder and Captain-General, who had led his country in heroic defiance of the French. When the Princess's father, James II, ascended the throne he sent Lely's most

---

[16] For the Dutch Gift see D. Mahon, *Burlington Magazine,* vol. xci (1949), pp.303–5, 349–50; vol. xcii (1950), pp.12–18, 238. The Dou is in the Mauritshuis (32); the Saenredam belongs to the Marquess of Bute (*Catalogue Raisonné of the Works by Pieter Jansz. Saenredam* (Utrecht, 1961), No.58). The important *Anthony and Cleopatra* by Jan de Bray, which includes the painter's self-portrait and is now at Hampton Court, was acquired in the reign of Charles II; so probably was the Van Aelst (No.92; Plate 72).

fashionable and successful follower, Willem Wissing of Amsterdam, over to Holland to paint portraits of William and his wife. Just over four years later the Protestant Wind blew William and his army to England and in 1689 a Dutch Prince and his English bride jointly ascended the throne. Thereafter the two countries were partners in the Grand Alliance, united in determination to oppose the aggressive menace of France.

A number of Dutch painters were at work in London in the later Stuart period. They had considerable influence on the development of painting in this country, especially in the development of genres other than the portrait. Cornelius Bol, Danckerts, Esselens, Schellinks, Leonard Knyff and Dirck van den Bergen in landscapes; Jan Wyck or Peter Tillemans in hunting scenes and battle-pieces; Knyff and Abraham Hondius in animal-pictures; Simon Verelst with flowers; Thomas Wyck with alchemists' dens and exotic harbours; Egbert van Heemskerck with scenes of 'Sots Paradice' or boorish carousals in the tradition of Adriaen van Ostade: such painters were helping to lay the foundations for the work by British artists in these fields in the eighteenth century. Of the immigrant Dutch artists at this period, none was more important or prolific than the Van de Veldes, father and son, who were taken under the protection of Charles II and the Duke of York soon after their arrival in this country late in 1672 or early in 1673. The King commissioned from the younger painter a picture of the *Royal Escape* (No. 41; Plate 68), the coal-brig in which he had escaped to France and which was fitted up after the Restoration as a smack or royal yacht. Both artists worked for the Duke of York on a set of eleven pictures of naval actions. The two finest in this set (Nos.18, 23; Plates 65, 66) have a spaciousness and atmosphere (what the artist himself called 'the air and the nature of its colour') which anticipate the finest of Monamy's, Brooking's or Samuel Scott's sea-pieces.

The qualities of high finish and ingenuity in certain types of Dutch painting intrigued English connoisseurs. Samuel Pepys, for example, was fascinated by a *trompe l'œil* in the style of Collier or Roestraeten, by the deceptive drop of dew on a leaf in a flower-piece by Verelst ('worth going twenty miles to see') or by the fascinating deceptions in an architectural perspective by Samuel van Hoogstraeten ('strange things to think how they do delude one's eye'). This delight in the ingenious and the highly finished

16

v Detail from Plate 15

vi Detail from Plate 16

is manifested in the admiration felt for little candle-light scenes, a genre which Dou developed (e.g., No.55; Plate 39) and which was exploited by his pupil, Godfried Schalcken, who enjoyed considerable success in London in the reign of William III. In one of the last portraits of the King[17] his bony face is lit by one of Schalcken's enormous candles.

When John Evelyn saw in 1660 the 'two rare pieces of Drolerie' by Dou which had been given to Charles II, he had described them as done 'so finely as hardly to be at all distinguished from *Enamail*'.[18] It was just this quality, however, which disgusted a critic and philosopher such as the 3rd Earl of Shaftesbury. He disliked the subject-matter which appealed to waggish collectors and bitterly attacked the decadent competence of a painter like Van der Werff: 'all false, bound up, glued, clung, candied, baked . . . minute . . . particularized . . . No sacrifice of under parts . . . no elevation . . . or sublime'. The Earl's outburst expresses the conventional classical tastes of the eighteenth century. By contrast the painter Jonathan Richardson wrote that the 'surprising Beauties' of Rembrandt were often overlooked, even by 'Lovers of Painting and Connoisseurs'; and he praised the merits of other Dutch painters as well.[19]

Frederick, Prince of Wales, the first of the Hanoverian dynasty to show a lively interest in the arts, formed a collection of Italian, Spanish, French and Flemish pictures, but seems to have owned only a small cabinet of Dutch pictures;[20] he may have acquired a Rembrandtesque *Portrait of a Girl*;[21] and it is conceivable that he also bought the splendid portrait by Frans Hals (No.5; Plate 10): a good example of the change, partly reflecting developments in

---

[17] There are versions in the Rijksmuseum (2140) and at Attingham.

[18] *Diary*, ed. E. S. de Beer (1955), vol. III, p.262.

[19] Shaftesbury's *Second Characters*, ed. B. Rand (1914), pp.165–6; *An Essay on the Theory of Painting* (ed. of 1725), pp.67–8, quoted by S. Slive, *Rembrandt and his Critics* (The Hague, 1953), p.151.

[20] The accounts of the Princess of Wales include, under 30 September 1753, 2s. to a man 'for Measureing the Dutch pickters, in the Wardrope' (Accounts of the Prince and Princess preserved in the Duchy of Cornwall Office, vol. xxv (1), f.54).

[21] Now at Buckingham Palace; it has recently been attributed to Drost. The Prince paid £18 for '1 Rainbrant' among pictures bought for him in France in 1735 (ibid., vol. VI (1), f.293). He sat to Hendrick van der Myn, who was paid on 4 September 1735 £63 for a portrait of the Prince (ibid., vol. v); the Prince's eldest sister had married William IV of Orange in 1734.

fashion, that comes over Hals's style in the 1630's and can be measured by comparing the sobriety of No.5 with the panache and gay colour of the *Laughing Cavalier* of 1624.[22] A small number of portraits by Hals seem to have been in England by the middle of the eighteenth century.[23] He was already admired for 'that strong-marked character of individual nature, which is so remarkable in his portraits, and is not found in an equal degree in any other painter'.[24] The portrait is first referred to at Buckingham House in the reign of George III. The King was a practical collector and his acquisitions, even the purchase of Consul Smith's collection in 1762, were made principally in order that Buckingham House, which he had bought for his Queen in 1761, should be worthily furnished with pictures. Joseph Smith had been established in Venice by 1709. His collection was particularly rich in Venetian eighteenth-century pictures, but as early as 1710 he and his partner had had business dealings in Amsterdam and he had managed to assemble a good collection of Dutch and Flemish pictures. They were ultimately hung by the King and Queen Charlotte at Kew and Buckingham House; many of them, in their distinctive Venetian frames, are still to be found in the royal collection. The pictures under Rembrandt's name in the Flemish and Dutch section of the lists of Smith's pictures include the *Rabbi* at Hampton Court and, probably, the *Young Man in a Turban* (No.7; Plate 37), although the measurements are given incorrectly in the lists and it is just conceivable that this panel had been in Charles II's collection as a *Self-portrait*. Smith also owned Rembrandt's *Deposition*, now in the National Gallery (43), and the superb *Concord of the State* in the Museum Boymans-Van Beuningen in Rotterdam (1717.)[25]

---

[22] S. Slive in *Frans Hals,* exhibition in Frans Halsmuseum, Haarlem, 1962 (26).

[23] E.g., ibid. (2, 9, 19, 20, 57).

[24] Sir Joshua Reynolds, *Discourses on Art*, ed. R. R. Wark (1959), p.109.

[25] A. Blunt and E. Croft-Murray, *Venetian Drawings ... at Windsor Castle* (1957), pp.19–23; Frances Vivian, 'Joseph Smith and Giovanni Antonio Pellegrini', *Burlington Magazine*, vol. CIV (1962), pp.330–3. A tantalizing reference is to 'A Storm' in the inventory of George III's pictures at Kew, *c.* 1800–5, said to be by 'C. Jordaens', which is later altered to 'An early work of Rembrandt', measurements given as 24½ × 36 in. In a slightly later inventory it is described as 'A Land Storm' on panel. Queen Charlotte owned two *Flower-pieces* by Van Huysum, which were in her sale at Christie's, 25 May 1819 (91, 92). George III, or possibly his father, bought the two landscapes at Hampton Court by Herman van Swanevelt.

Among such familiar names in Smith's Dutch and Flemish list as Wouwermans, Berchem, Mieris, Weenix, Steen, Van de Velde, Ostade and Dou, Frans Post's *villagio Americano* (No.51; Plate 53) stands out as a delightful little oddity, probably painted in Haarlem after Post's return in 1644 from Brazil, where he had been in the service of Count John Maurice of Nassau-Siegen. After he got back to Holland Post continued to paint Brazilian subjects – the first views by a European artist of the New World – from sketches made on the spot. Smith's Post had belonged to the decorative painter Giovanni Antonio Pellegrini, whose collection, after his death in 1741, had been acquired by Smith. Pellegrini had worked in Holland, where he had probably found a picture '*con Donna alla Spinetta*'. It had been in the famous sale at Amsterdam in 1696 of twenty-one of Vermeer's pictures, the property of a Delft publisher, Jacobus Dissius. It appears with an attribution to Frans van Mieris in Smith's Dutch and Flemish list as 'A Woman playing on a Spinnet in presence of a Man seems to be her father.' Almost by accident, therefore, George III bought one of the finest Dutch pictures in the royal collection: Vermeer's *Lady at the Virginals* (No.10; Plate 14). It was thought, at a later date, to be too bad for Frans, and was given to Willem van Mieris. Mrs Jameson, who found it attributed to Eglon van der Neer, preferred to retain the attribution to the younger Mieris.[26] In criticizing the artist for placing the figures too far back, Mrs Jameson was unconsciously pointing to important aspects of Vermeer's style towards the end of his career: the contrast between dark foreground and more brightly lit background, and the recording of perspective across a wide angle. The reflection of the lady's face in the mirror, in which one can also see the bottom of Vermeer's easel, tells us something of Vermeer's method of working. It is impossible to define the elements of symbolism and illustration, to assess the precise nature of the allusions to love and music that may be synthesized in the picture, or to be sure that we are moving in what one writer has described as 'un monde de galanterie élégante et à demi-secrète'; but it is surely hardly adequate to call the picture by its old title: *The Music Lesson.*

---

[26] *A Handbook to the Public Galleries of Art* (1842), pt. 1, p.249: 'very awkward and tasteless, the figures being too far back'.

George IV, as Prince of Wales, Regent and King, was, after Charles I, the most distinguished and prodigal royal collector. He bought French furniture, china and tapestry, and French, Flemish and Dutch pictures. In the disposition of his beautiful possessions at Carlton House George IV followed the practice established by the great French collectors of the eighteenth century who had frequently combined their French furniture and decoration with Dutch and Flemish seventeenth-century paintings, often set in frames made for them in Paris. French collectors had begun to buy Dutch pictures at the end of the seventeenth century. Louis XIV owned a Rembrandt in 1683. In the eighteenth century Dutch pictures were the rage in France and were commanding high prices. A number of superb collections were formed. During the French Revolution they were dispersed. The protracted strain of a long war led also to the dispersal of a number of Dutch and Belgian cabinets of pictures. Hundreds of pictures came to England, owing to the comparatively tranquil conditions in which the London art-market could flourish and thanks to the energies of a number of dealers and importers. The flood of pictures which passed into this country from the Continent, roughly between the outbreak of the French Revolution and the accession of George IV, permanently enriched the artistic heritage of Great Britain. Buchanan wrote of the upheavals in France and Italy that 'from these sources have our principal riches in art been derived'; the import of so many great works of art from the Continent to England had aroused a taste for the acquisition of works of art which had lain dormant since the days of Charles I. Famous collections of Dutch and Flemish pictures were brought over to London to be exhibited and sold: the Orléans collection in 1792, the Calonne collection in 1795, the collection of the Greffiers Fagel, sold in London in 1801, for example. The last-named contained the little Pot (No.61; Plate 3) of the family of Charles I. Enterprising and well-placed travellers and merchants profited from the confusion of the times to buy pictures on the Continent which they could bring back to London, often in difficult and even dangerous conditions, and sell at a substantial profit. John Trumbull, for instance, bought pictures in Paris during the Revolution from a number of important French collections and sold them on his return at Christie's in February 1797. Bryan, a merchant who had a special knowledge of Dutch collections, was buying in Holland when the country was overrun by the French revolutionary armies. He sold the pictures in London in May 1798. In Paris he bought heavily at the Robit sale in 1801; the exhibition and sale of these pictures in London were particularly rich in fine Dutch and Flemish pieces. Bryan, in short, secured 'many of the best pictures of the Dutch school that are now in England'. No less important were the importations of pictures by Delahante and, above all, Buchanan who brought over many Dutch pictures from French collections and was active in the Low Countries right down to 1817.

George IV, and rival collectors like the Duke of Bridgewater, the 1st Marquess of Bute, Lord Grosvenor, Lord Lansdowne and Sir Robert Peel, reaped a rich harvest in these hectic years; and the King's Dutch pictures came almost entirely from celebrated French collections and Dutch cabinets. Rembrandt's *Christ and the Magdalen at the Tomb* (No.15; Plate 8), which he bought from Lafontaine in 1819, had belonged to the Empress Josephine at Malmaison; earlier it had been in the Landgrave's collection at Kassel; and it is first recorded in a Dutch collection in Leiden in 1721, when it was bought for the famous Röver collection in Delft. One of the King's Schalckens (No.48; Plate 32), which had belonged to Louis XVI, had been noted in a cabinet in The Hague early in the eighteenth century. Some of his pictures had been in the most celebrated of French eighteenth-century collections of Dutch pictures, the Duc de Choiseul's: Dou's famous *Hachis d'Oignons* (No.56; Plate 40) and *Grocer's Shop* (No.57; Plate 41) and one of the Du Jardins (No.47; Plate 62), for example. The *Hachis d'Oignons* had also been in the Prince de Conti's famous collection of Dutch and Flemish pictures. Of the many Dutch collections from which pictures came into George IV's possession, the most important were perhaps those formed by Gerret Braamcamp in his house on the Heerengracht in Amsterdam and, slightly later, by Jan Gildemeester Jansz. on the same waterway. The Braamcamp collection was rich in painters who were universally popular in the eighteenth century and were to be well represented at Carlton House: Berchem, Both, the Ostades, Metsu, Steen, Ruisdael, Wouwermans, Dou, Du Jardin, Willem van Mieris, Potter. Very good examples by Adriaen van de Velde (Nos.32, 36; Plates 59, 60) and Potter (No.40; Plate 28) found their way from the Heerengracht to Pall Mall. The Potter passed, in the interval, into the Gildemeester collection. From this superb collection the most highly prized items came into the King's hands: Cuyp's *Evening Landscape* (No.17; Plate 20), Rembrandt's *Shipbuilder* (No.22; Plate 5) and Ter Borch's *Letter* (No.26; Plate 15). The two De Hoochs (Nos.11, 14; Plates 12, 13) and Steen's *Morning Toilet* (No.38; Plate 16), among the last of George IV's purchases, had apparently never previously left the Low Countries.[27]

Like many serious collectors George IV was continually improving the quality of his collection. A long list of pictures cleaned for him, as Prince of Wales, by George Simpson in 1793-5 contains only a handful of pictures, apart from royal portraits, which are still in the royal collection. The artists' names include Van de Velde, Poelenburgh, Du Jardin, Wouwermans, Schalcken, Peeters, Lairesse, Adriaen van Ostade, Bramer and Rembrandt.[28] On 26 May 1814 the Regent sent to Christie's a group of pictures from his 'Old Collection' with fifteen pictures from those he had bought from Sir Thomas Baring;[29] they appeared in a sale, 'selected from a distinguished cabinet', at Christie's on 29 June 1814. The formation of the Prince's collection of European pictures, as we know it today, was begun at, or soon after, the turn of the century.[30] Pictures were bought in the trade from dealers such as Delahante and John Smith, and at auction, where the bidding was often done for the Prince by his principal adviser on pictures, Lord Yarmouth, who succeeded as 3rd Marquess of Hertford in 1822 and is chiefly remembered as the prototype

---

[27] W. Buchanan, *Memoirs of Painting,* 2 vols. (1824), provides the best account of the flow of pictures into England at this period; vol. II, pp.349-60, contains a lively account of one of his operations, in which he was determined to out-manoeuvre some Parisian rivals. Much material is to be found in John Smith, *A Catalogue Raisonné of the Works of the Most Eminent Dutch, Flemish, and French Painters,* eight parts (1829-37) and *Supplement* (1842). For modern studies of two important Dutch collections, see Clara Bille, *Der Tempel der Kunst of Het Kabinet van den Heer Braamcamp* (Amsterdam, 1961) and C. J. de Bruyn Kops, 'De Amsterdamse Verzemelaar Jan Gildemeester Jansz., *Bulletin van het Rijksmuseum* (1965).

[28] P.R.O., H.O. 73, 23.

[29] Benjamin Jutsham's Day-book of receipts and deliveries at Carlton House, preserved in the office of the Surveyor of The Queen's Pictures.

[30] For an account of the principal sources for our knowledge of George IV's collection, see O. Millar, *The Later Georgian Pictures in the Collection of H.M. The Queen* (1969), pp. l-lii. The earliest inventory is that made by Michael Bryan, dated 1816, but with additions up to 1 November 1830. The Day-books of receipts begin at 31 December 1806. If a picture in the 1816 inventory does not appear in the Day-books, it can be assumed to have been acquired before 31 December 1806.

of Thackeray's vicious Lord Steyne. Lord Yarmouth was a man of taste who shared and encouraged the Prince's taste for Dutch pictures.[31] When, for example, he came away from the sale of John Humble's pictures at Christie's on 11 April 1812, he sat down to write to the Regent: 'I bought for your Royal Highness this morning the Fishermen for 430 Gui[ns] & the Coup de Pistolet for 390 Gui[ns] – the Horse fair being by Peter not Philip Wouv:[ns] I left at 230, Lord Mulgrave bought it – I thought his Lordships bidder a puffer & having seen the picture sold last year by Phillips for Eighty I did not like to Treble the sum.'[32] On 26 April 1812 he again reported that he had bought pictures for the Prince at Christie's, presumably on the previous day: 'I enclose the catalogue with the prices of some of the best pictures marked.'[33] Sir Charles Long, later Lord Farnborough, also played an active part in the formation of the Prince's collection. William Seguier, who was closely involved in the arrangement and care of the pictures and in 1820 succeeded Benjamin West as Surveyor, also bought pictures for the Prince. The cleaning and repair of the pictures were often entrusted to George Simpson and frames for some of the Dutch pictures were made by Edward Wyatt.[34]

The Prince's earliest purchases were probably fairly modest: good, but not outstanding, pictures by Adriaen and Isack van Ostade;[35] and pictures by such painters as Eglon Hendrik van der Neer and Willem van Mieris whose narrative content – 'the true stamp of nature' – and high finish would have appealed to the Prince.[36] In the Prince's inventory of 1816 one of the paintings by Van der Neer was said to be 'like Schalcken'; he had by then acquired two examples (Nos.48, 85; Plates 32, 75) by this painter.

---

[31] His own are overshadowed at Hertford House by the superb examples acquired by his successor.

[32] Windsor, Royal Archives, Georgian 26918. The *Coup de Pistolet* is No.42 below; the *Fishermen* by Teniers is at Buckingham Palace.

[33] Ibid., Georgian 26924.

[34] Simpson's bill for work done in 1811 included five guineas for cleaning and repairing the superb Adriaen van de Velde (No.37; Plate 23); the frames for the Hondecoeters (e.g., Nos.27, 30; Plates 31, 74) were made by Edward Wyatt (ibid., 27830; Jutsham's book of deliveries, f.63).

[35] Including Isack's *Milkmaid*. On 14 May 1805 he paid Philip Hill £367 10*s*. for 'a Beautiful Cabinet Picture' by Ostade (ibid., Georgian 26826).

[36] The *Fruiterer's Shop* by Mieris (No.89; Plate 50) is probably the 'Beautiful Cabinet Picture by Mieris' which the Prince bought from Hill for £315 on the same day.

On 4 March 1805 he bought, among other pictures from John Parke, a *Breeze* by Willem van de Velde for £315;[37] it is still at Buckingham Palace. The Prince was not interested in still life painting. Only a signed *Still Life* by Willem Heda, bought as by Willem Kalf, seems to belong to this period of the Prince's career as a collector and in 1814 he sold a pair of pictures by Rachel Ruysch. In this early stage of his appreciation of Dutch pictures one can see that the subject-matter in some of them would have fitted in with other parts of his collection. The enthusiasm for military subjects, which led to the accumulation of a mass of military drawings and arms of all kinds, probably explains the Prince's buying an early battle-piece by Wouwermans and (from Dighton in March 1810) a feeble barrack-room scene in the style of Troost.[38] His fine English sporting pictures, by Gilpin, Garrard, Ben Marshall, Schwanfelder, Chalon and Stubbs, might have seemed to the Prince to be in the tradition of hawking scenes by Wouwermans, Cuyp's *Trooper with a Grey Horse*, a picture of a sportsman on horseback, bought at Christie's in 1803 as a Cuyp of the Prince of Orange, the *Stag-Hunt* by Hackaert and Berchem which is now in the National Gallery (829), or the superb *Negro Page* by Cuyp,[39] which had been bought at Lord Rendlesham's sale in 1806. At the end of his life George IV spent much of his time at the King's (or Royal) Lodge in the Great Park at Windsor. He sent down to this retreat his finest pictures of the country-house variety. These were principally his British pictures – his best sporting pieces, genre scenes by Bird, Collins, Wilkie and Mulready, his Gainsborough of the Duke and Duchess of Cumberland – but he realized that they could well hang in company with a little picture, now attributed to Lodolf de Jongh,[40] of elegant company in the gardens of a mansion and with the set of three unusual pictures by Hondecoeter (e.g., Nos.27, 30; Plates 31, 74) of a gentleman with his hounds and horses painted against a background of his castle and gardens. The pictures had been bought by Walsh Porter at Lady Holderness's sale at Christie's on 6 March 1802 and are among the Prince's earliest purchases

---

[37] Ibid., 26825.

[38] At Buckingham Palace and Hampton Court respectively.

[39] The Cuyps are at Buckingham Palace.

[40] At Windsor.

24

VII Detail from Plate 23

VIII Detail from Plate 27

in the collection as we know it today. There is, moreover, a link between the Prince's patronage of living painters and his admiration of the Dutch and Flemish genre painters of the seventeenth century. Lord Mulgrave had said in 1806 that he believed Wilkie would 'go beyond Teniers, Ostade and all who had preceded Him'. Wilkie's early style had been formed on a close study of such painters and of David Deuchar's imitations of them. Lord Mulgrave thought that Wilkie gave to his genre scenes more 'thought & abstraction' than would be found in their seventeenth-century prototypes. William Collins praised the refinement and humour which Wilkie had brought to his treatment of such subjects; he admired the technical skill of the Dutch painters, but he thought their subject-matter was often 'gross, vulgar and filthy'. This prudishness recalls Lairesse's strictures on pictures of 'tobacco smokers . . . dirty children on their pots, and other things more filthy and worse'; it might have been prompted by a picture such as Adriaen van Ostade's *Peasant Family* (No.33; Plate 9).[41]

During the second decade of the century the Prince made some of his most important purchases. His collection of landscapes was enlarged with such masterpieces as the Ruisdael (No.19; Plate 25); a number of pictures by Wouwermans (who had been so popular in the previous century and was still Smith's 'incomparable artist') including the *Pistol-Shot* (No.42; Plate 22), which had originally been brought over by Delahante; Adriaen van de Velde's exquisite *Departure for the Chase* (No.37; Plate 23); the *Hawking Party* by Wijnants (No.45; Plate 56); and the *Sportsmen* by Potter (No.34; Plate 51). The Wijnants is a reminder of Gainsborough's early love for this painter. A group of five Dutch pictures, with attributions to Wouwermans, Cuyp, Lingelbach and Maes, was bought at Christie's on 26 January 1811 for a total of £765 9s. On 7 February 1811 £2625 was paid to William Harris for five pictures. They included the *Sportsmen* by Potter, two *Calms* by Willem van de Velde and the *Approach to the Town of Veere* by Van der Heyden (No.52; Plate 67).[42] On 12 June 1811 the Prince bought a superb group of pictures at the Lafontaine

---

[41] O. Millar, op. cit., pp. xxxvii–viii; Farington described the portraits at Carlton House of the Prince's family by Stroehling as 'painted in a Vanderwerfe manner'.

[42] Windsor, Royal Archives, Georgian 26881, 27087.

sale at Christie's. Adriaen van de Velde's *Shepherd and Shepherdess* (No.32; Plate 59) is one of the richest pictures by this artist in the royal collection; recent cleaning has revealed the lovely soft atmosphere of the *Hayfield* by Wouwermans (No.31; Plate 58); and the Both (No.12; Plate 21) is a magnificent example of his mature classical landscapes, suffused in golden sunlight and nostalgia for the Campagna, complex in design: a pattern for classical landscape painting for many generations to come. Adriaen van Ostade's *Peasant Family* (No.33; Plate 9) is the most beautiful of the genre scenes of this type acquired by the Prince. It demonstrates, once again, the quality and condition of the pictures which he bought. In the same sale the Prince bought his first Rembrandt, the *Shipbuilder and his Wife* (No.22; Plate 5). It could be argued that it was the greatest picture in the Prince's collection. Strongly lit, deeply perceptive of the personalities of the old couple, most beautifully preserved, it is an example of the dramatic range of invention which Rembrandt displayed in the portraits commissioned from him in his early years in Amsterdam. 1811 was something of an *annus mirabilis* in the annals of the royal collection. In 1812 the Prince bought the small Ter Borch (No.64; Plate 48) in which the quiet tonality is subtly adjusted to the mood in which the lovers meet.

These purchases were a prelude to the Prince's most important *coup*: the acquisition in 1814 of eighty-six pictures from the collection of Sir Thomas Baring, of which some had been acquired by his father, Sir Francis Baring. The pictures arrived at Carlton House on 6 May 1814. A handful of these were Flemish (principally a fine group of pictures by Teniers); a few pictures were sent in to Christie's to be auctioned; but the remaining pictures compose one of those purchases *en bloc* which have from time to time transformed the look of the royal collection. The cabinet pictures included the little Pot (No.61; Plate 3) of the royal family in 1632 in which the formal grandeur of early baroque court portraiture is presented on an almost miniature scale and with a miniaturist's delicacy of touch. Among the genre scenes are two panels by Adriaen van Ostade (Nos.54, 63; Plates 44, 43) of exceptional quality; in one (No.54; Plate 44) an elderly couple seem to be dressed in sixteenth-century costume, reminiscent of portraits by Maerten van Heemskerk. Ostade lacks the characteristic bite and sparkle – the sincerity, too – of Jan Steen, whose

Tavern Interior (No.25; Plate 17) is a splendid example of his powers as a craftsman, his restless sense of design and, incidentally, his importance for a painter like Wilkie. His *Twelfth Night Feast* (No. 49; Plate 46), with its quirky combination of symbolism and riot, is painted in a subtler range of colour. The finest of the interior scenes among the pictures bought from Baring is the *Letter* by Ter Borch: a miraculous example of Ter Borch's mature style with its extremely refined and perceptive presentation of fabrics and human relationships alike, concentrated with characteristic poise within an interior created with rare delicacy in the handling of light and atmosphere. The fall of light and the range of colour perhaps indicate the influence of Vermeer. Looking at the treatment of the big hanging chandelier it is curious that the Prince did not keep Van Eyck's *Arnolfini* group, which was on offer at Carlton House until April 1818. Metsu's *Self-portrait* (No.58; Plate 42) is a good example of a touch that is broader and less subtle than Ter Borch's. The gradual decline in Dutch painting, a decline in moral and psychological intensity which goes with undiminished technical virtuosity, can be traced from Dou's *Hachis d'Oignons* of 1646 (No.56; Plate 40) down to the charming trivia of Van der Werff (No.87; Plate 47) or the metallic finish and coarse feeling of Willem van Mieris (Nos.88, 89; Plates 49, 50). The *Hachis d'Oignons* is the earliest dated example of Dou's favourite convention, in which figures, engaged in some daily pursuit or household task, are seen as if through an open window. It is also a fine example of his delicate tone, quiet mood, and concentrated attention to still life.

No less remarkable are the landscapes which came into the collection among the Baring pictures. The landscapes by Adriaen van de Velde are, once again, of very fine quality. They include two Italianate scenes of shepherds and flocks (Nos.36, 62; Plates 60, 61) and the atmospheric, unforced, little scene on the *Coast at Scheveningen* (No.46; Plate 24). In the same class is Van der Heyden's *Country House by a Canal* (No.50; Plate 30). In a grander vein is Hobbema's richly painted *Wooded Landscape* (No.24; Plate 54). There is a particularly fine display of works by the Italianate landscape painters[43] whose works had been so much admired by con-

---

[43] For this group, see W. Stechow, *Dutch Landscape Painting of the Seventeenth Century* (1966), ch. VIII.

noisseurs and critics since the seventeenth century and had, in England, influenced such painters as Gainsborough. Within the royal collection there are reminders in the work of Schalch and De Loutherbourg of the pervading influence of Both and Berchem. Poelenburgh, the founder of the group, had probably been in Rome as early as 1617. His little landscape on copper (No.43; Plate 26), which epitomises his Arcadian view of the Italian scene, was painted in Rome and is closely related to a pair of landscapes in the Louvre, of which one is dated 1620. At this point in his career Poelenburgh's style is particularly delicate and close to that of Breenbergh to whom, indeed, the little copper was attributed while it was at Carlton House; both painters were influenced by such painters as Elsheimer, Bril and Tassi, whose works they would have encountered in Rome. Despite an individual breadth of tone and softness of form, Poelenburgh remained to a great extent a Mannerist. Berchem, in the second generation of Dutch Italianate landscape painters, was in Italy in the 1640's. He was deeply influenced by Both, who is believed to have returned to Utrecht from Rome in 1641. Among the landscapes by Berchem from the Baring collection, the late *Mountainous Landscape* (No.28; Plate 64) is still steeped in Both's vision of the Campagna. In the exquisite *Italian Landscape* (No.44; Plate 27) there is almost a premonition of early Corot in the clarity of Both's vision. The landscape is bathed in shimmering Italian sunlight which strengthens the supposition that Berchem revisited Italy in the 1650's. The handling of paint on the figures and the white horse is suggestive of Gainsborough. They would not be out of place ambling through Cornard Wood. One of Du Jardin's little pictures of boys looking after cows (No.59; Plate 29) is Italianate in atmosphere; the other (No.47; Plate 62) is like a more delicately handled Paulus Potter. Potter himself was represented in the Baring collection by the *Young Thief* (No.40; Plate 28) with its characteristic mixture of strident handling in the foreground and unexpected delicacy in the background. The chief glory of the Baring landscapes are the three Cuyps: the little *Horsemen* (No.53; Plate 55) which could be tentatively dated *c*.1650 on the basis of style rather than costume; the wonderful *Evening Landscape* (No.17; Plate 20), flooded in an evening light of liquid gold – Turner's 'golden colour of ambient vapour'; and the *Passage-Boat* (No.9; Plate 18) with its rich handling in the sky and water. No painter is more expressive of that 'unique silence' which is so marked a characteristic of Dutch painting of the golden age.[44]

The Baring collection also included a fine late *Dead Game* by Jan Weenix (No.65; Plate 73); a *Calm* (No.21; Plate 19) by the younger Van de Velde, which is a classic example of the soft light and carefully planned disposition of the vessels which mark his best works in this vein; a sad little picture (No.91; Plate 69) of two pigs awaiting slaughter, which went under Potter's name and bore a false signature, but is in fact a signed work by Cornelis Saftleven; a fairly early Wouwermans (No.39; Plate 57) in which the rather broad handling and opaque texture still show something of the influence on him of Pieter van Laer; and the *Self-portrait* by Rembrandt (No.35; Plate 7).

Certain pictures were acquired by the Prince through exchanges. In May 1814 he gave William Harris, in exchange for Rubens's *Landscape with St George*, two pictures by Van Huysum from the Baring collection and an Adriaen van Ostade which he had bought from Harris three years earlier. Harris received in addition £500 to make up the purchase price of £2,700. In July 1819 the Prince gave Lafontaine two paintings by Mieris, with a Steen, a Wouwermans, the *Stag-Hunt* by Hackaert, a Van der Heyden and a Teniers in exchange for a Dou and a *Horse-Fair* by Wouwermans.[45] On 6 November 1819 there arrived at Carlton House from the Custom House three pictures which Lafontaine was offering to the Prince. He determined to keep only Rembrandt's *Christ and the Magdalen at the Tomb* (No.15; Plate 8), one of the most beautiful renderings of a sacred subject by the painter who was, among Northern artists, the supreme interpreter of the Bible. The panel has the fine quality of Rembrandt's early works on this scale, but there is a new richness of texture and the morning light on the landscape create a powerful emotional effect. It is probable that as early as 1660 Rembrandt had been praised for the majestic effect he had created in the dim light and limitless depths of the tomb. To secure this picture the Prince handed over to Lafontaine two *Calms* by Van de Velde, an *Alchemist* by Teniers and an *Herodias* attributed to Matsys.

Carlton House by now must have presented a splendid appear-

---

[44] S. Slive, *Rembrandt and his Critics* (The Hague, 1953), p.2.

[45] Jutsham's Day-books of receipts and deliveries, ff. 150, 153, 307, 318, 320.

ance: a 'happy combination of splendid materials tastefully arranged'. The Dutch and Flemish pictures were principally hung, on the state floor, in the Bow or Rose Satin Drawing-Room, the Blue Velvet or Audience Room (it is here that the *Shipbuilder and his Wife* (Plate IX) was hung), and the Blue Velvet Closet or Little Blue Room; and, in the lower apartments, in the Lower Vestibule, the Golden Drawing-Room or Colonnade Room, the Bow Room, the Ante-Room to the Dining-Room and the Dining-Room itself. In each of Henry Holland's gorgeous rooms the pictures were carefully placed to complement the magnificent furniture and works of art, hanging in new frames against backgrounds of rose-coloured satin damask, scarlet cloth, scarlet flock, and scarlet silk, or dark blue velvet set off in light peachblossom. The visitor was further dazzled by a blaze of gilding and glass.[46] Only a comparatively small part of the Prince's collection was on show in these rooms. The inventory of pictures at Carlton House in 1816 lists 136 in the principal apartments; a further 67, including very good Dutch pieces, were in the attics, which included the Prince's bedroom. Nearly 250 more were in store, presumably because there was no room for them to be incorporated in the state rooms.

With such riches already under his roof, it is understandable that the Prince bought less avidly for the rest of his life. He was by now disinclined to buy collections *en bloc*. When, in 1819, Buchanan informed Sir Charles Long that the Aynard collection, one of the finest in Paris, could probably be purchased by the Prince, he found the list 'too general' and was only anxious to acquire works which he felt his collection 'actually wanted'; he bought only the *Farm at Laeken* by Rubens. Another French collection offered by Buchanan, that of Comte Morel de Vindé, was not thought to be important enough by the Prince or his advisers.[47] He paid a thousand guineas for the *Interior of a Grocer's Shop* by Dou (No.57; Plate 41), probably to Thompson Martin in 1817. This marks perhaps the culmination in England of the cult of a painter who had been so highly prized in the eighteenth

---

[46] Something of the lustre of these rooms is conveyed in the views of them by C. Wild, published in W. H. Pyne's invaluable description of Carlton House in his *History of the Royal Residences*, vol. III (1819). See Plate IX.

[47] Buchanan, op. cit., vol. II, pp.371–2.

IX *C. Wild*
The Blue Velvet Room
at Carlton House (1816)

x *Douglas Morison* The Picture Gallery at Buckingham Palace in 1843

century and was to be described by Smith as 'a perfect master of all the principles of art; which, united with consummate skill and labour, enabled him to produce the most perfect specimens that ever came from the easel of a painter'. George IV paid more for the *Grocer's Shop* than for Rembrandt's *Lady with a Fan*; his taste 'led him to appreciate, in a high degree, the productions of this captivating Master'.[48] It is more elaborate in design than the *Hachis d'Oignons* of twenty-six years earlier. The scale has become larger; there is a view through to a well-filled background: and the setting has become more ornate, with an elaborate proscenium draped with a curtain and a ledge below decorated with a bas-relief. These elements were imitated by Dou's followers during the decline from the heroic age of Dutch painting: they are clearly seen in Mieris's *Fruiterer's Shop* (No.89; Plate 50) of 1732. In 1818 George IV bought pictures by Van der Werff and Du Jardin from Lafontaine; in 1819 Lord Yarmouth bought for him a *Candle-light* by Schalcken from the collection of Lord Charles Townshend; a *Storm* by Willem van de Velde the younger was acquired from Delahante in 1820; a Steen and an Aert van der Neer were among the King's last purchases.[49] He bought also in these later years four outstandingly important Dutch pictures. On 7 July 1821 he bought from Delahante Steen's *Morning Toilet* (No.38; Plate 16): a panel of exquisite quality and with subtle allusions, in skull, lute, music-book and cherub's head, to the conflict between the varied fortunes of earthly life and the assurance of heavenly bliss. On 27 April 1825 the King bought from John Smith the *Card-Players* by De Hooch (No.11; Plate 12), a masterpiece from the painter's finest period; in May 1829 he acquired another beautiful piece (No.14; Plate 13) by the same painter. After the great days of the Baring collection the finest Dutch picture bought by George IV is, however, Rembrandt's *Lady with a Fan* (No.13; Plate 11), bought for him by Lord Yarmouth at Lord Charles Townshend's sale on 4 June 1819. It makes an absorbingly interesting contrast, in the handling, the thoughtful perception of character, the contemplative glance, and the softened light, with the *Shipbuilder and his Wife* painted eight years earlier.

---

[48] Windsor, Royal Archives, Georgian 26994; Smith, op. cit., vol. 1 (1829), p.3.

[49] All these late purchases are still in the collection.

There is no indication where these last purchases were going to be placed. As early as October 1821 Farington was reporting that the new King was feeling 'a dislike' to Carlton House and a desire to move into Buckingham House. By September 1826 Carlton House had been stripped of its contents. The King's collection of pictures was sent to St James's Palace. By July 1830 they had been deposited in store at 105 Pall Mall.[50] It had been convenient to the King to lend to the British Institution two large consignments of pictures which formed by themselves the annual exhibitions of Old Masters in 1826 and 1827. In earlier years he had been a generous lender to the Institution. When Waagen first visited England in 1835 he found the late King's pictures still in store in five rooms in Pall Mall, where it was not easy to see them well. He expressed the pious hope that William IV would present them to the National Gallery. Many were intended for 'Buckingham House, the new Royal Palace in London'; and in March 1836 the pictures were 'on removal' to Buckingham Palace. By the end of the reign of William IV, or early in the reign of Queen Victoria, and certainly by the summer of 1839, George IV's great Dutch and Flemish collection, with the exception of such pictures as had earlier gone down to Windsor, were set up in the new Picture Gallery at Buckingham Palace. The King himself, in other words, never again saw them properly displayed as a collection after he had taken the decision to abandon Carlton House.[51]

In 1841 a printed catalogue was issued of Queen Victoria's pictures in Buckingham Palace. In the Picture Gallery no fewer than 185 pictures were hanging. Almost all were from George IV's collection and the majority were Dutch, mixed with a number of Flemish pictures and a sprinkling of British, German, Italian and French pieces. Mrs Jameson, who published an account of the

---

[50] Windsor, Royal Archives, Georgian 35846, 32710.

[51] G. F. Waagen, *Works of Art and Artists in England* (1838), vol. II, pp.348–57; *Athenaeum*, 5 March 1836; *The Girlhood of Queen Victoria,* ed. Lord Esher (1912), vol. II, p.223, recording her discussion with Melbourne on 31 July 1839 'of the beautiful pictures in the Gallery here . . . of their being all Dutch, which we agreed was a low style; our preferring the Italian Masters'. However, she acquired the Willaerts (No.86; Plate 4) in 1858.

'Private Gallery' of the Queen,[52] thought the Gallery too lofty and 'the light not well contrived for such small and delicate pictures'. A water-colour of the Picture Gallery in 1843 (Plate x)[53] shows the pictures tightly packed up the walls, in some places four deep and for the most part in heavy frames of a Regency design. By 1850 every picture in the Gallery had been put, presumably at the Prince Consort's instructions, into uniform frames of a particularly unfeeling design and tone, made by William Thomas.[54] Since the last war the Dutch pictures have been rearranged. They hang less densely in the Picture Gallery and are dispersed in other parts of the Palace. Many of Thomas's frames have been discarded and the pictures placed either in dark frames of the type in which many of them would originally have been hung or in gilded frames of a more elaborate design, suggesting how they would have been framed by French or English collectors in the eighteenth century. During the same period many of the pictures have been cleaned.

Mrs Jameson was not far wrong when she described Queen Victoria's Gallery as 'certainly the finest gallery of this class of works in England'. The royal collection does not, inevitably, contain works by those painters or from those artistic movements in Holland which have been brought to light by modern scholarship and are in tune with modern taste. Even by the end of George IV's reign, his tastes may have seemed a little old-fashioned. His Dutch pictures were all by the favourites of the French eighteenth-century: the painters, in other words, tackled by Smith in his volumes. In 1823 Hazlitt wrote in admiration of the naturalistic qualities of Van Goyen. Constable, with Turner and Crome, venerated Ruisdael, Hobbema, Cuyp and Willem van de Velde; but he declared in a lecture in 1836 that Both and Berchem had 'produced a bastard style of landscape'. After the lecture he advised a collector in the audience to burn his Berchems.[55]

---

[52] *Companion to the Most Celebrated Private Galleries of Art in London* (1844), pp.1–76. Visitors were only admitted when the Queen was away from the Palace and by an order from the Lord Chamberlain. Mrs. Jameson had, incidentally, been given the figure of £24,000 as the price paid by George IV for the Baring collection.

[53] By Douglas Morison in the Royal Library.

[54] Thomas was paid £919 for 185 new gilt frames (E. Joy, 'The Royal Victorian Furniture-Makers, 1837–87', *Burlington Magazine,* vol. cxi (1969), p.682).

[55] *Collected Works* of Hazlitt, ed. A. R. Waller and A. Glover, vol. ix (1903), p.36; *John Constable's Discourses*, ed. R. B. Beckett (1970), pp.34, 56.

Salomon van Ruysdael's little *River Landscape* (No.90: Plate 52), which appears in the royal collection early in Queen Victoria's reign, brings a breath of fresh, damp, air straight from the skies and waterways of Holland into the sultry Italianate atmosphere of the painters Constable despised. The royal collection can demonstrate more clearly than any other three main phases in the history of the appreciation of Dutch painting in this country: the time when works by painters in the young Republic were brought over the North Sea as esteemed diplomatic gifts, and discerning envoys and connoisseurs were keen to secure works by living painters and to invite the painters themselves to try their fortunes in London; the 'Age of Observation', when cultural links between the two countries were so strong and when Dutch artists were working to such effect in England under the later Stuarts; and the revolutionary period, when fashionable taste for Dutch pictures was gratified so lavishly that the 'celebrated cabinets of Holland' were emptied and the acquisitions made by George IV and his contemporaries 'comprise some of the most exquisite and valuable productions' of the Dutch school. Owing to the acquisitiveness of Charles I and George IV, the quality of the Dutch pictures in The Queen's collection sets a standard for the assessment of the technical ability of certain Dutch painters which is only attained elsewhere in this country (and on this scale) in the other famous collections built up in the first part of the nineteenth century: in the Duke of Wellington's collection at Apsley House, at Hertford House, in the Duke of Sutherland's collection, in the Fitzwilliam Museum and, at the National Gallery, in the pictures assembled by Sir Robert Peel and acquired by the Gallery in 1871.

More important than the lessons that can be learnt from the royal collection in the history of English taste are the intense pleasure that can be derived from the Dutch pictures themselves and the evidence they so abundantly provide of the economic prosperity and the cultural vitality of the Dutch Republic in the seventeenth century, its prosperous peasantry and unostentatious nobility, its seas and waterways, its quiet domestic life. The paintings, produced over a comparatively short period, are indeed the Republic's most splendid achievements. In three of the seven United Provinces, and within a territory comprising little more than sixty square miles of this small and watery land, a quantity of painters and schools of painting flourished to an extent unsurpassed anywhere else and at any period in the history of art. This prodigal activity and the widespread popularity of painting in seventeenth-century Holland impressed one English traveller as early as 1640:

As For the art off Painting and the affection off the people to Pictures, I thincke none other goe beeyond them, there having bin in this Country Many excellent Men in thatt Facullty, some att presentt, as Rimbrantt, etts, All in generall striving to adorne their houses, especially the outer or street roome, with costly peeces, Butchers and bakers not much inferiour in their shoppes, which are Fairely sett Forth, yea many tymes blacksmithes, Coblers etts., will have some picture or other by their Forge and in their stalle. Such is the generall Notion, enclination and delight that these Countrie Native(s) have to Paintings.[56]

The fascination of Dutch painting of the seventeenth century lies in its consistently brilliant and delicate technique; in its restraint, a quality seen to perfection in Ter Borch and Cuyp; and in an all-embracing realism, a passionate interest in everyday happenings and in the appearance of the Dutch countryside and of the Dutch towns and cities. Dutch painters made masterpieces out of scenes of daily life because they captured its essential spirit and recognized its painterly qualities. This we see especially clearly in the work of painters like Adriaen van Ostade or Steen; in the patient study of the richness and variety of stuffs; and, above all, in variations in the rendering of light: in the sunlight effects of Adriaen van de Velde, Cuyp or Both, or in Van der Heyden's soft atmosphere as well as in the works of such masters as Vermeer, De Hooch and Ter Borch. 'One would wish to be able to convey to the reader some idea of that excellence, the sight of which has afforded so much pleasure; but as their merit often consists in the truth of representation alone, whatever praise they deserve, whatever pleasure they give when under the eye, they make but a poor figure in description.'[57] Reynolds wrote with his usual intelligence; but he does not take note of that intense,

---

[56] *The Travels of Peter Mundy in Europe and Asia 1608–1667*, ed. Sir R. C. Temple, vol. IV (1925), *Hakluyt Society*, second series, vol. IV (for 1924), p.70. In the summer of 1641 John Evelyn was in Holland and found the annual fair at Rotterdam 'so furish'd with pictures (especially Landscips, and Drolleries, as they call those clownish representations) as I was amaz'd' (*Diary*, ed. E. S. de Beer (1955), vol. II, p.39).

[57] *A Journey to Flanders and Holland in the year 1781*, first published with Reynolds's *Works* (1797).

although rigidly controlled, emotional quality in so many Dutch painters which raises to the highest level works, even of the so-called 'Little Masters', which might, without this poetic quality, seem at first sight to deal with subjects of small significance.

O.N.M.

A volume on the Dutch pictures in the new Catalogue Raisonné *of the royal collection is being prepared by Mr Christopher White. The notes on the pictures in this small book have been kept brief in expectation of a fuller treatment in Mr White's volume. Literary references have been, in the main, limited to the standard or more recent publications and to those which will lead the student on to more material. Mr Michael Robinson has identified the subjects in Van de Velde's* Sea-Fights.

The English reader will find the best account of Dutch seventeenth-century painting in J. Rosenberg, S. Slive, E. H. Ter Kuile, Dutch Art and Architecture 1600 to 1800 *(1966), with a superb bibliography; and is also recommended to read W. Stechow,* Dutch Landscape Painting of the Seventeenth Century *(2nd edn., 1968). A mass of information is to be found in N. MacLaren's catalogue,* The Dutch School *(National Gallery, 1960).*

1 *Hendrick Ter Brugghen* A Bass Viol Player with a Glass (No.1)

2 *Gerrit van Honthorst* George, Duke of Buckingham, with his Family (No.29)

3 *Hendrick Gerritsz. Pot*
Charles I, Henrietta Maria
and Charles, Prince of Wales
(No.61)

4 *Adam Willaerts* The Embarkation of a Prince (No.86)

5 *Rembrandt* The Shipbuilder and his Wife (No.22)

6 *Rembrandt* The Artist's Mother (No.4)

7 *Rembrandt* Portrait of the Artist (No.35)

8 *Rembrandt* Christ and the Magdalen at the Tomb (No.15)

9 *Adriaen van Ostade* A Peasant Family at Home (No.33)

10 *Frans Hals* Portrait of a Man (No.5)

11 *Rembrandt* The Lady with a Fan (No.13)

12 *Pieter de Hooch* The Card-Players (No.11)

13 *Pieter de Hooch* A Courtyard in Delft (No.14)

14 *Johannes Vermeer* A Lady at the Virginals (No.10)

15 *Gerard Ter Borch* The Letter (No.26)

16 *Jan Steen* The Morning Toilet (No.38)

17 *Jan Steen* The Interior of a Tavern (No.25)

18 *Aelbert Cuyp*
The Passage-Boat (No.9)

19 *Willem van de Velde the Younger*
Ships in a Calm (No.21)

20 *Aelbert Cuyp* An Evening Landscape (No.17)

21 *Jan Both* Landscape with
S. Philip baptizing the Eunuch
(No.12)

22 *Philips Wouvermans* The Pistol-Shot (No.42)

23 *Adriaen van de Velde* The Departure for the Chase (No.37)

24 *Adriaen van de Velde*
The Coast at Scheveningen
(No.46)

25 *Jacob van Ruisdael*
The Windmill (No.19)

26 *Cornelis van Poelenburgh* Shepherds with their Flocks (No.43)

27 *Nicolaes Berchem* An Italian Landscape (No.44)

28 *Paulus Potter* The Young Thief (No.40)

29　*Karel Du Jardin*
A Shepherd Boy asleep (No.59)

30 *Jan van der Heyden*
A Country House (No. 50)

31 *Melchior de Hondecoeter*
A Gentleman on Horseback
(No.27)

32 *Godfried Schalcken* Seven Persons playing a Game (No.48)

Abbreviations

Bredius=*The Paintings of Rembrandt*, ed. A. Bredius (Vienna, 1935; English ed. 1937).

Bauch=K. Bauch, *Rembrandt Gemälde* (Berlin, 1966).

Gerson=H. Gerson, *Rembrandt Paintings* (1968).

Bredius/Gerson=A. Bredius, *Rembrandt. The Complete Edition of the Paintings,* revised by H. Gerson (1969).

Haak=B. Haak, *Rembrandt, His Life, His Work, His Time* (New York, n.d. (1969)).

H. de Groot=C. Hofstede de Groot, *Beschreibendes und kritisches Verzeichnis der Werke der hervorragendsten holländischen Maler des XVII. Jahrhunderts,* 10 vols. (Esslingen a N., 1907–28), English translation of vols. 1–8 (1908–27).

Rosenberg, Slive, Ter Kuile=J. Rosenberg, S. Slive, E. H. Ter Kuile, *Dutch Art and Architecture 1600 to 1800* (1966).

Welcker=C. J. Welcker, *Hendrik Avercamp ... en Barent Avercamp* (Zwolle, 1933).

Puyvelde=L. van Puyvelde, *The Dutch Drawings ... at Windsor Castle* (1944).

Catalogue

Hendrick Ter Brugghen (1588(?)–1629)

1 A Bass Viol Player with a Glass *Plate 1*

Oil on canvas: $41\frac{1}{8} \times 33\frac{1}{2}$ in. Signed and dated: *HTBrugghen fecit 1625* (initials in monogram). Acquired by Charles I and placed in the Long Gallery at Whitehall: '. . . a drunken swaggering laffing fellowe in blewe Slasht Sleeves. and in an old leathorn buff coate houlding in his left hand a Vyall de gambo . . .' (B. Nicolson, *Hendrick Terbrugghen* (1958), pp. 12–14, 70–1 (No.A35)). Nicolson points out the appearance of the same bass viol in a copy of a lost work by Ter Brugghen (his plate 55b) and states that the glass held by the musician is an allusion to the pleasures of Taste. The bravo's costume appears in a number of Ter Brugghen's pictures of the 1620's.

Hendrick Gerritsz. Pot (c.1585–1657)

2 A Startling Introduction *Plate 34*

Oil on panel: $24\frac{5}{8} \times 30\frac{1}{4}$ in. Signed: *HP* (in monogram). In the collection of Charles I whose brand is on the back of the panel.

Painted at the same period as No.61, perhaps in 1632, when the artist was in London. The subject-matter has not been satisfactorily explained. In 1649 the picture was described as 'A sould^r. makeinge a strange. posture to a. duitch. ladye done by Pott.' In the inventory of Queen Anne's pictures a suggestion was first made that the figures were the Black Prince and the Countess of Salisbury, a theory discounted by Walpole ('it is probably some foreign story'). It was suggested in the nineteenth century that the picture represented a scene from a play. A version at Ingatestone, which bears Pot's monogram, is described as the 5th Earl of Derwentwater (the Jacobite) descending a chimney to make his tenth, and successful, proposal of marriage to the Countess of Newburgh. The lady is clearly threatening to commit suicide, but the gentleman has presumably been in the room some time: his cloak and sword are on a chair on the left. The significance of the partly de-flowered rose on the floor, the hound savaging the lady's lap-dog, the glass of wine and the belt on the table remains to be discovered. The carved heraldic decoration over the fireplace seems to be Dutch rather than English in style. In the version at Ingatestone the shield can be seen to bear a lion rampant.

Adriaen Hanneman (c.1601–1671)

3 Peter Oliver (c.1594–1648) *Plate 35*
Oil on canvas: 30 × 22 in. Probably acquired by Charles II from Peter Oliver's widow soon after the Restoration.

Probably painted *c*.1632–5. Peter Oliver was one of the most distinguished miniature-painters at the early Stuart court. His family was of Huguenot origin (O. Millar, *The Tudor, Stuart and early Georgian Pictures in the Collection of Her Majesty The Queen* (1963), No.214).

Rembrandt (1606–69)

4 The Artist's Mother *Plate 6*
Oil on panel: 24⅛ × 18⅝ in. One of the three pictures presented to Charles I by Sir Robert Kerr, later Earl of Ancram; on the back of the panel are the CR brand and a label, applied under the eye of Charles I's Surveyor, which records the present from Sir Robert (J. G. van Gelder, 'Rembrandt and his Circle', *Burlington Magazine*, vol. XCV (1953), p. 37).

Painted *c*.1629. Rembrandt's mother, Neeltje van Suydtbroeck, had married Harmen Gerritsz. van Rijn in 1589. She bore him nine children and died in 1640. She was possibly too young to be identified with the aged subject of a number of studies of an old woman etched and painted by Rembrandt in his early years. In this study Rembrandt may have intended her to be representing a prophetess. The panel had been used by him earlier, the other way up, for a study of an old man. A number of copies, some in miniature, are recorded. The great age of the sitter has often caused her to be described as the centenarian Countess of Desmond, an identification which was also attached to the original from the time of Queen Anne until *c*.1815 (H. de Groot, No.688; Bredius, No.70; Bauch, No.251; Gerson, pp.18, 198, 490 (37); Bredius/Gerson, pl.66; Haak, pp.46–7).

Frans Hals (c.1580(?)–1666)

5 Portrait of a Man *Plate 10*
Oil on canvas: 46 × 35½ in. Inscribed: *AETAT SVÆ 36/AN 1630*. Perhaps acquired by George III or by his father, Frederick, Prince of Wales (H. de Groot, No.286; W. R. Valentiner, *Klassiker der Kunst* (Stuttgart, Berlin, Leipzig, 1923), 84; N. S. Trivas, *The Paintings of*

Frans Hals (1941), p.38 (No.37); S. Slive, *Frans Hals,* vol. II (1970), pl.109, No.68). Cleaning (1970/1) revealed that No.5 had been over-painted, particularly heavily in the costume. The fall of drapery below the sitter's elbow and an area of drapery below the waist on the right had been painted out. The inscription had been strengthened.

Daniel Mytens (c.1590–1647)

6 Portrait of the Artist *Plate 38*
Oil on panel: 26⅞ × 23⅛ in. Presumably painted for Charles I *c.*1630; the panel bears on the back the King's brand. A native of Delft, Mytens was in London by 1618. Until he was overshadowed by Van Dyck he produced a succession of accomplished official portraits of Charles I (O. Millar, *The Tudor, Stuart and early Georgian Pictures in the Collection of Her Majesty The Queen* (1963), No.114; O. Ter Kuile, 'Daniel Mijtens', *Nederlands Kunsthistorisch Jaarboek*, vol. XX (1969), pp.82–3.

Rembrandt (1606–69)

7 A Young Man in a Turban *Plate 37*
Oil on panel: 25¾ × 20 in. Signed and dated: *RHL.1631* (initials in monogram). Possibly No.26 in the list of Dutch and Flemish pictures acquired by George III with the collection of Consul Smith in 1762: 'Rembrandt. His own Portrait in a Turban on Board', although the measurements are given in the list as 25 × 25 in.; but it could perhaps be identified with a so-called *Self-portrait* by Rembrandt which can perhaps be traced back to an entry, in Charles II's inventory of the pictures in Whitehall, for a *Self-portrait* by 'Rembranke', measurements given as 24 × 20 in. (H. de Groot, No.354; Bredius, No.142; Bauch, No.136; Gerson, No.106; Bredius/Gerson, pl.126).

Adriaen Hanneman (c.1601–1671)

8 William III (1650–1702) when Prince of Orange *Plate 70*
Oil on canvas: 51¾ × 41½ in. Signed and dated: *Anº 1664. / Adr. Hanneman. F.* One of two identical portraits (the other is also in the royal collection) for which Hanneman was paid 500 gulden on 26 June 1664. The portraits had been painted for the Prince's grandmother, Queen Henrietta Maria, and his aunt by marriage, Anne Hyde, Duch-ess of York. They may have been commissioned by the Prince's other grandmother, Amalia van Solms (O. Millar, *The Tudor, Stuart and early Georgian Pictures in the Collection of Her Ma*ᵉ*esty The Queen* (1963), No. 209).

Aelbert Cuyp (1620–91)

9 The Passage-Boat *Plate 18*
Oil on canvas: 49 × 56¾ in. Signed: *A cüyp*. Purchased by George IV
with the Baring collection (91) in 1814 and placed in the Audience
Room at Carlton House.

A passage-boat approaching a landing-stage, its approach heralded by
a drummer on board. The river is almost certainly the Merwede at
Dordrecht, where Cuyp had a house. The costumes of the figures perhaps suggest a date *c*.1650 (H. de Groot, No.637).

Johannes Vermeer (1632–75)

10 A Lady at the Virginals with a Gentleman *Plates IV, 14*
Oil on canvas: 29 × 25¼ in. Signed: *IVMeer* (initials in monogram).
Recorded in a sale in Amsterdam, 16 May 1696 (6), when the subject
was described as a young lady playing on the virginals in a room and a
gentleman listening. Bought with the collection of Giovanni Antonio
Pellegrini by Consul Smith and sold to George III in 1762 as by Frans
van Mieris.

Generally dated *c*.1665–70. The gentleman's costume would fit with
such a dating. The painting hanging on the right of the design
(Vermeer's signature is on the frame) is a version of a *Roman Charity*.
On the lid of the virginals, which is almost identical with an instru-
ment made in 1620 by Andries Ruckers the Elder, is the inscription:
MVSICA. LETITIAE CO(ME?)S/MEDICINA. DOLOR(IS?).
The bass viol on the floor behind the lady may have been played by the
gentleman in concert with the virginals (L. Gowing, *Vermeer* (1952),
pp.37–40, 52–5, 119–27; Rosenberg, Slive, Ter Kuile, pp.122–3,
pl.96b; see also, for example, A. P. de Mirimonde, 'Les Sujets Musicaux
chez Vermeer de Delft', *Gazette des Beaux-Arts* (Paris, January 1961),
pp.29–50, or A. Berendsen on Vermeer in *Delft* (Antwerp etc., 1962),
pp.89–103).

Pieter de Hooch (1629–after 1684 (?))

11 The Card-Players *Plate 12*
Oil on canvas: 30 × 26 in. Signed and dated: *P.D.H./1658*. Bought by
George IV from John Smith on 27 April 1825, formerly in the Wal-
raven, Doekscheer, Quarles van Ufford and Hulswit collections, all
in Amsterdam.

It has been suggested, not very convincingly, that this masterpiece
from De Hooch's finest period, when he was working in Delft, is a

companion piece to the *Interior* in the National Gallery (834), in which the maidservant in the background is apparently painted from the same model as the lady playing cards (H. de Groot, No.254; W. R. Valentiner, *Klassiker der Kunst* (Stuttgart, Berlin, Leipzig, 1929), 51; *Masterpieces of the Dutch School*, Mauritshuis, The Hague, 1948 (3); Rosenberg, Slive, Ter Kuile, p.124).

Jan Both (c.1618(?)–1652)

12 **Landscape with S. Philip baptizing the Eunuch** *Plate 21*
Oil on canvas: 50½×63 in. Signed: *JBoth* (initials in monogram). Bought by George IV at the Lafontaine sale, Christie's, 12 June 1811 (57), and placed in the Audience Room at Carlton House; formerly in the Court van der Voort-Backer and Smeth van Alphen collections (H. de Groot, No.9; *Ideal and Classical Landscape*, National Museum of Wales, 1960 (11)). The scene is perhaps unusual in Both's *œuvre* for the introduction of a Biblical subject, taken from Acts VIII. 26–39, in the foreground.

Rembrandt (1606–69)

13 **Agatha Bas (1611–58): the Lady with a Fan** *Plate 11*
Oil on canvas: 41½×33 in. Signed and dated: *Rembrandt f/1641* and inscribed *Æ.29*. Agatha Bas, eldest daughter of Dirck Jacobsz. Bas, a burgomaster of Amsterdam, married Nicolaas van Bambeeck in 1638. Rembrandt painted companion portraits of them which were imported into England in 1814 by the dealer Nieuwenhuys and sold at Christie's, 29 June 1814 (76, 77). The portrait of the lady was later sold to Lord Charles Townshend, at whose sale (Robins, 4 June 1819 (32)) it was bought by George IV. The portrait of Nicolaas van Bambeeck is in Brussels (I. H. van Eeghen, *Een Amsterdamse Burgemeestersdochter van Rembrandt in Buckingham Palace* (Amsterdam, 1958)).

There are clear traces of alterations by Rembrandt during painting: in the position of the left hand and in the silhouette of the dress at the bottom (H. de Groot, No.860; Bredius, No.360; Bauch, No.501; Rosenberg, Slive, Ter Kuile, p.64; Gerson, pp.88, 497 (233); Bredius/Gerson, pl.281).

Pieter de Hooch (*1629–after 1684 (?)*)

14 A Courtyard in Delft at Evening, with a Woman spinning *Plate 13*
Oil on canvas: 27¼×21 in. Signed: *P.D.HOOCH*. Bought by George
IV at the T. Emmerson sale by Phillips, 2 May 1829 (152); recorded on
the art-market in Amsterdam in 1819 and London in 1824.

A masterpiece, probably painted *c*.1656, from the period when De
Hooch was working in Delft and producing his finest work. In the
background are the towers of the Town Hall and Nieuwe Kerk at
Delft (H. de Groot, No.292; W. R. Valentiner, *Klassiker der Kunst*
(Stuttgart, Berlin, Leipzig, 1929), 45; *Masterpieces of the Dutch School,*
Mauritshuis, The Hague, 1948(2)).

Rembrandt (*1606–69*)

15 Christ and the Magdalen at the Tomb *Plate 8*
Oil on panel: 24×19½ in. Signed and dated: *Rembrandt f^t/1638*. On the
back of the panel is a manuscript copy of a poem addressed to Rembrandt by his friend Jeremias de Decker. In the poem, published in
De Hollantsche Parnas of 1660, the writer praises a painting of this
subject, done 'by the outstanding Mr. Rembrandt van Rijn for H. F.
Waterloos'. Recorded in the collection of Willem van der Goes in
Leyden in 1721, when it was bought by Valerius Röver of Delft; acquired by the Landgrave of Hesse for the Gallery at Kassel, but removed in 1806 and secured for the Empress Josephine's collection at
Malmaison; acquired by George IV from Lafontaine in 1819.

Two drawings survive in which Rembrandt worked out combina-
tions of the principal elements in the final design (O. Benesch, *The
Drawings of Rembrandt*, vol. III (1955), Nos.537, 538). There are perhaps
traces of alteration by Rembrandt in the painting of the interior of the
cavern-like tomb. Rembrandt's design may have been in Isack van
Ostade's mind in composing a picture, now at Englefield, of Christ as
the Gardener (H. de Groot, No.142; Bredius, No.559; S. Slive, *Rembrandt and his Critics* (The Hague, 1953), pp.46, 174; Bauch, No.66;
Rembrandt, Rijksmuseum, 1956 (34); Gerson, pp.54, 492 (82); Bredius/
Gerson, pl.473; Haak, pp.154, 323).

Sir Peter Lely (*1618–80*)

16 Mary II (1662–94) when Princess *Plate 71*
Oil on canvas: 48½×38½ in. Probably painted *c*.1672, some five years
before the Princess's marriage to the Prince of Orange (No.8). The
portrait was possibly painted for the Princess's parents, James II

76

and his first wife; but it does not appear in the records of the royal collection before the reign of Queen Anne, when it was hanging in the Queen's Dining-Room at Windsor. The Princess is dressed as Diana, drawing her bow and followed by a greyhound (O. Millar, *The Tudor, Stuart and early Georgian Pictures in the Collection of Her Majesty The Queen* (1963), No.249).

Aelbert Cuyp (1620–91)

17 An Evening Landscape with Figures and Sheep *Plate 20*
Oil on canvas: 40 × 60½ in. Signed: *A. cüyp*. Purchased by George IV with the Baring collection (37) in 1814 and placed in the Bow Room on the state floor at Carlton House. Formerly in the Van Slingeland and Gildemeester collections.

. The figures perhaps suggest a date in the 1650's. The landscape has been stated to be near the Rhine (H. de Groot, No.432; Rosenberg, Slive, Ter Kuile, p.159, pl.142).

Willem van de Velde the Younger (1633–1707)

18 An Engagement at Sea: an English Merchant Ship attacked by three Spanish Privateers, one of which is the 'Sangte Michal' *Plate 65*
Oil on canvas: 49⅝ × 72 in. Signed and dated: *W Vande Velde 1677*. Nos.18 and 23 form part of a set of eleven pictures of naval actions, painted by the Van de Veldes (at least one is by the father), for James II when he was Duke of York. They are recorded in his collection at Whitehall.

Jacob van Ruisdael (1628 or 1629(?)–1682)

19 The Windmill *Plate 25*
Oil on canvas: 31 × 40¼ in. Signed: *JvRuisdael* (initials in monogram). Purchased by George IV at the Walsh Porter sale at Christie's, 14 April 1810 (8), and placed in the Little Blue Room at Carlton House; formerly in the collection of the Earl of Halifax (H. de Groot, No.173, 197b; J. Rosenberg, *Jacob van Ruisdael* (Berlin, 1928), No.114). Probably painted *c.*1655.

Jan Steen (*1625 or 1626–1679*)

20 The Interior of a Tavern with Peasants eating and drinking and a Couple dancing *Plate 45*
Oil on canvas: 24½ × 29½ in. Signed: *JSteen* (initials in monogram). Purchased by George IV with the Baring collection (17) in 1814 and placed in the Ante-Room on the ground floor at Carlton House (H. de Groot, No.597). Probably painted *c*.1660.

Willem van de Velde the Younger (*1633–1707*)

21 Ships in a Calm *Plate 19*
Oil on panel: 23½ × 28 in. Purchased by George IV with the Baring collection (51) in 1814 and placed in the Dining-Room at Carlton House; formerly in the Smeth van Alphen collection, Amsterdam (H. de Groot, No.198). Painted in Holland, presumably *c*.1665.

Rembrandt (*1606–69*)

22 Jan Rijcksen or Harder (1560/1–1637) and Griet Jans: the Shipbuilder and his Wife *Plates II, III, 5*
Oil on canvas: 45 × 66½ in. Signed and dated: *Rembrandt. f:/1633*. Jan Rijcksen, a very prosperous Amsterdam shipbuilder, Master-Shipbuilder to the East India Company, married Griet Jans in 1584. The signature which appears on the open book and the name on the note held in his wife's hand could be read as his; and the inventory of the contents of the family house on the Rapenburg in Amsterdam, drawn up in 1659 after the death of Jan Rijcksen's son Cornelis, includes: *Een schilderije van des overledens vader en moeder geschildert door Rembrant van Reen* (I. H. van Eeghen, 'Jan Rijcksen en Griet Jans', *Amstelodamum* (Amsterdam, June–July 1970), pp.121–7). The picture was later in the Gildemeester and Smeth van Alphen collections in Amsterdam (see C. J. de Bruyn Kops, 'De Amsterdamse Verzamelaar Jan Gildemeester Jansz.', *Bulletin van het Rijksmuseum* (1965), pp.111–12). It was bought in the Lafontaine sale at Christie's, 12 June 1811 (63), and placed in the Audience Room at Carlton House (H. de Groot, No.933; Bredius, No.408; *Rembrandt,* Nationalmuseum, Stockholm 1956 (13); Bauch, No.532; Gerson, p.494 (139); Haak, p.89; *Rembrandt 1669–1969*, Rijksmuseum, 1969 (2)).

Willem van de Velde the Younger (1633–1707)

23 An Engagement at Sea: an English Merchant Ship or Indiaman capturing a Spanish Privateer, the 'Sangte Domyngo', and driving off two others *Plate 66*

Oil on canvas: 49½ × 72 in. Signed and dated: *W,V,Velde 1682*. See No.18.

Meyndert Hobbema (1638–1709)

24 A Wooded Landscape with Travellers and Beggars in a Lane
Plate 54

Oil on panel: 24½ × 35¼ in. Signed and dated: *M Hobbema/f. 1668*. Purchased by George IV with the Baring collection (4) in 1814 and placed in the Prince Regent's Ante-Room at Carlton House (H. de Groot, No.78); G. Broulhiet, *Meindert Hobbema* (Paris, 1938), No.274: W. Stechow, *Dutch Landscape Painting of the Seventeenth Century* (1968), pp.78–9).

Cleaning and restoration (1956) revealed considerable *pentimenti* in the figures, which are remarkably loosely painted and appear to have been slightly reduced in importance by the painter. The picture is very close stylistically to a painting in the National Gallery (2571) and to the *Wooded Landscape* of 1667 in the Fitzwilliam Museum (49).

Jan Steen (1625 or 1626–1679)

25 The Interior of a Tavern with a Violin Player *Plate 17*

Oil on canvas: 32½ × 27½ in. Signed: *JSteen* (initials in monogram). Bought by George IV from Joseph Waring in April 1818; formerly in the Clicquet-Andrioli collection in Amsterdam (H. de Groot, No.532; W. Martin, *Jan Steen* (Amsterdam, 1954), p.54).

Painted *c*.1665. The artist himself is seen seated, laughing, in front of the fire.

Gerard Ter Borch (1617–81)

26 The Letter *Plates V, 15*

Oil on canvas: 32⅛ × 26⅞ in. It is conceivable that there are faint traces of a signature on the letter. Purchased by George IV with the Baring collection (45) in 1814 and placed in the Dining-Room at Carlton House. Formerly in the Beaujou (Paris) and Gildemeester (Amsterdam) collections.

Painted soon after 1660. The page is probably a portrait of the artist's stepbrother, Moses Ter Borch (1645–67). The girl reading the letter is probably a portrait of his stepsister Gesina (1631–90) (S. J. Gudlaugsson, *Gerard Ter Borch* (The Hague), vol. I (1959), pp.126–30, pl.169; vol. II (1960), pp.174–5, No.169; C. J. de Bruyn Kops, 'De Amsterdamse Verzamelaar Jan Gildemeester Jansz.', *Bulletin van het Rijksmuseum* (1965), pp.82–3).

Melchior de Hondecoeter (1636–95)

27 A Gentleman on Horseback outside the Gate of a Country House
Plate 31

Oil on canvas: $31\frac{1}{2} \times 38\frac{1}{4}$ in. Signed and dated: *M. Hondekoe . . ./A°1687;* the signature is obscure and may have been strengthened at a later date. The three pictures in the set, of which two are in the exhibition, were in George IV's collection by 1816; they were sold in Lady Holderness's sale at Christie's, 6 March 1802 (26–28). They were sent from the Drawing-Room at Carlton House to Warwick House on 26 August 1816 and on 31 May 1822 were sent down to the King's Lodge in Windsor Great Park.

The three canvases (see also No.30) were presumably commissioned by the owner of the house, who is seen mounted on a superb cream whose quarters are decorated with his owner's crest under an elaborate coronet. In No.27 two more horses are seen, a skewbald and a bay, with a group of beagles and greyhounds. On the left is a glimpse of an elaborate formal garden.

Nicolaes Berchem (1620–83)

28 A Mountainous Landscape with Peasants driving Cattle and Sheep *Plate 64*

Oil on canvas: $27\frac{1}{4} \times 32\frac{1}{8}$ in. Signed: *Berchem*. Purchased by George IV with the Baring collection (21) in 1814 and placed in the Prince Regent's Ante-Room at Carlton House (H. de Groot, No.493).

A version of the composition is in the Musée Fabre at Montpellier; another is in Riga. The design probably dates from *c*.1670–80.

Gerrit van Honthorst (1590–1656)

29 George Villiers, 1st Duke of Buckingham (1592–1628), with his Family *Plates I, 2*

Oil on canvas: $52 \times 75\frac{7}{8}$ in. The Duke is seated beside his Duchess, Lady Catherine Manners, daughter of the 6th Earl of Rutland, whom he had married in 1620. She holds their infant son George, later the

2nd Duke of Buckingham (1628–87), who stretches out his hands to reach an apronful of flowers held up by his sister, Lady Mary Villiers (1622–85).

Painted for the King in the summer of 1628. The Duke was assassinated on 23 August 1628; his son had been born on 30 January. The portrait of the Duke was extensively copied (see D. Piper, *Catalogue of Seventeenth-Century Portraits in the National Portrait Gallery* (1963), p.40). Miniature copies of the Duke's head were also made, e.g., in enamel by Jean Petitot; an example, dated 1640, is at Welbeck, and a miniature of this type is worn by the Duchess on a mourning bow in a portrait by Van Dyck (H. Braun, *Gerard und Willem van Honthorst* (Göttingen, 1966), pp.222–4).

Melchior de Hondecoeter (*1636–95*)

30 Grooms with Horses, a Grey and a Dark Bay, at the Back of a Country House *Plate 74*

Oil on canvas: 31¼ × 37¾ in. Signed and dated: *M.D. Hond…/168(6?)*; the signature is damaged and has been strengthened.

A companion picture to No.27. The groom wears the livery which appears in the other picture, and the house, from which two figures observe the scene, is perhaps also the same, seen from a different point. In the distance the owner of the estate is seen walking with his wife on a terrace. His ornamental birds include a flamingo, turkey and crowned crane.

In the third picture in the series, which is obscurely signed, a Negro groom in the same livery assists a riding-master (?) at the *manège*; it shows a string of magnificent creams.

Philips Wouwermans (*1619–68*)

31 The Hayfield *Plate 58*

Oil on canvas: 26½ × 31 in. Signed: *PHLS . W* (*PHLS* in monogram). Purchased by George IV at the Lafontaine sale at Christie's, 12 June 1811 (61), and placed in the Bow Room on the state floor at Carlton House; formerly in the Smeth van Alphen collection, Amsterdam (H. de Groot, No.940).

Adriaen van de Velde (1636–72)

32 A Shepherd and a Shepherdess with their Flocks by a Stream
Plate 59
Oil on canvas: $25\frac{1}{4} \times 30\frac{7}{8}$ in. Signed and dated: *A.V.Velde f/1668*.
Bought for George IV at the Lafontaine sale at Christie's, 12 June 1811
(60), and placed in the Bow Room on the state floor at Carlton House;
formerly in the Braamcamp, Doekscheer and Smeth van Alphen collections in Amsterdam (H. de Groot, No.211; Clara Bille, *De Tempel der
Kunst of Het Kabinet van den Heer Braamcamp* (Amsterdam, 1961),
catalogue, pp.58, 124–5 (No.236)).

Adriaen van Ostade (1610–85)

33 A Peasant Family at Home *Plate 9*
Oil on panel: $18\frac{3}{8} \times 16\frac{3}{8}$ in. Signed and dated: *Av. Ostade./1668* (the *Av.*
in monogram). Bought for George IV at the Lafontaine sale at
Christie's, 12 June 1811 (59), and placed in the Bow Room on the state
floor at Carlton House; formerly in the Smeth van Alphen collection
in Amsterdam (H. de Groot, No.460). There are alterations in painting
in the area of the doll and the mother's arms.

Paulus Potter (1625–54)

34 Two Sportsmen outside a Tavern *Plate 51*
Oil on panel: $20\frac{3}{4} \times 17\frac{1}{4}$ in. Signed and dated: *Paulus Potter . f :1651*.
Bought by George IV from William Harris, 7 February 1811, and
placed in the Bow Room on the state floor at Carlton House; pre-
viously in the Randon de Boisset and Rendlesham collections (H. de
Groot, No.5).
Recent cleaning revealed considerable alterations in the form of the
trees in the hedge behind the sportsmen.

Rembrandt (1606–69)

35 Portrait of the Artist *Plate 7*
Oil on panel: $27\frac{5}{8} \times 23$ in. Signed and dated: *Rembrandt ft./164[7?]*
Purchased by George IV with the Baring collection (53) in 1814. The
final digit of the date is obscure, but the portrait is generally dated
c.1645. Rembrandt altered the shape of his hat in painting. It was
originally a small, flat, beret which was replaced by this flamboyant
bonnet of a vaguely sixteenth-century character which at one stage
may have been even larger and possibly sported a feather. A drawing

in the Lehmann collection is closely related to this portrait (Benesch, No.434) (H. de Groot, No.555; Bredius, No.37; *Rembrandt*, Rijksmuseum, 1956 (51); Bauch, No.319; Gerson, p.498 (253); F. Erpel, *Die Selbstbildnisse Rembrandts* (Berlin, 1967), pp.166–7, 174); Bredius/Gerson, pl.33).

Adriaen van de Velde (*1636–72*)

36 Shepherdesses with their Flocks in a Glade *Plate 60*
Oil on canvas: 26⅛ × 31 in. Signed and dated: *A.V.Velde : f./1664*.
Purchased by George IV with the Baring collection (43) in 1814 and placed in the Prince Regent's Ante-Room at Carlton House; formerly in the Braamcamp and Gildemeester collections in Amsterdam (H. de Groot, No.97; Clara Bille, *De Tempel der Kunst of Het Kabinet van den Heer Braamcamp* (Amsterdam, 1961), catalogue, pp.57, 124 (No.234); C. J. de Bruyn Kops, 'De Amsterdamse Verzamelaar Jan Gildemeester Jansz.', *Bulletin van het Rijksmuseum* (1965), p.111).

37 The Departure for the Chase *Plates VII, 23*
Oil on panel: 19⅞ × 18¾ in. Signed and dated: *A. V. Velde. f 1666*.
Bought by Lord Yarmouth for George IV at Lord Rendlesham's sale, Christie's, 28 May 1810 (32), and placed in the Bow Room on the state floor at Carlton House; formerly in the Choiseul-Praslin collection (H. de Groot, No.154).

Jan Steen (*1625 or 1626–1679*)

38 The Morning Toilet *Plates VI, 16*
Oil on panel: 25⅞ × 20⅞ in. Signed and dated: *JSteen*. (initials in monogram)/*1663*. Bought from Delahante by George IV in July 1821; formerly in the Kappeyne (Amsterdam) and Verhulst (Brussels) collections (H. de Groot, No.340).

The scene is viewed through an archway. On the ledge in the foreground rest conventional *Vanitas* symbols in opposition to the cherub's head at the top of the arch, which probably symbolizes heavenly, as opposed to earthly, joys. There is a variant of the design, without the architectural framework, in the Rijksmuseum (2250–A6) (W. Martin, *Jan Steen* (Amsterdam, 1954), pp.46–7; *Jan Steen*, Mauritshuis, 1958–9 (25); Rosenberg, Slive, Ter Kuile, p.136).

Philips Wouwermans (1619–68)

39 The Camp Farrier *Plate 57*
Oil on panel: 14¾ × 12¾ in. Purchased by George IV with the Baring collection (65) in 1814 and placed in the room next to the Dining-Room at Carlton House; formerly in the De Bruyn collection, Amsterdam (H. de Groot, No.130). Probably painted c.1650.

Paulus Potter (1625–54)

40 The Young Thief *Plate 28*
Oil on panel: 20½ × 30½ in. Signed and dated: *Paulus. Potter. f. 1649.* Purchased by George IV with the Baring collection (47) in 1814 and placed in the Bow Room on the state floor at Carlton House; formerly in the Braamcamp, Van der Marck, Randon de Boisset and Gildemeester collections (H. de Groot, No.90; Clara Bille, *De Tempel der Kunst of Het Kabinet van den Heer Braamcamp* (Amsterdam, 1961), catalogue, pp.40, 111 (No.168); C. J. de Bruyn Kops, 'De Amsterdamse Verzamelaar Jan Gildemeester Jansz.', *Bulletin van het Rijksmuseum* (1965), pp.101, 111).

Willem van de Velde the Younger (1633–1707)

41 The Royal Escape *Plate 68*
Oil on canvas: 25 × 30 in. Signed: *W.V.V.* Probably commissioned by Charles II c. 1675; recorded in the collection of James II: 'A Little sea piece, with the bark in it, that carried the King to France'.

The *Surprise* had been a Brightelmstone coal-brig. The owner, Nicholas Tattersall, had taken Charles II over to France from Shoreham on 15 October 1651 after his flight from Worcester. After the Restoration the *Surprise* was fitted up as a smack or royal yacht and renamed the *Royal Escape*.

Philips Wouwermans (1619–68)

42 The Pistol-Shot *Plate 22*
Oil on panel: 19½ × 17½ in. Signed: *PHILS. W* (*PHILS* in monogram). Bought by Lord Yarmouth for George IV at the Humble sale at Christie's, 11 April 1812 (62), and placed in the Bow Room on the state floor at Carlton House; formerly in the Nogaret, Tolozan and Heathcote collections (H. de Groot, No.859).

Cornelis van Poelenburgh (*1586(?)–1667*)

43 Shepherds with their Flocks in a Landscape with Ruins *Plate 26*

Oil on copper: 12½ × 15¾ in. Signed: *C.P.* Purchased by George IV with the Baring collection (28) in 1814 and placed in the Bow Room on the ground floor at Carlton House. Painted in Rome *c.*1622. On the right of the composition is the Temple of Castor and Pollux (E. Schaar, 'Poelenburgh und Breenbergh in Italien . . .', *Mitteilungen des Kunsthistorischen Institutes in Florenz,* vol. IX, part I (Florence, August 1959), pp.25–54; *Nederlandse 17e Eeuwse Italianiserende Landschapschilders,* Centraal Museum, Utrecht, 1965 (12)).

Nicolaes Berchem (*1620–83*)

44 An Italian Landscape with Ruins and Figures: two Shepherds with their Flocks and a Peasant Woman on a White Horse
Plates VIII, 27

Oil on panel: 13 × 17⅜ in. Signed and dated: *CBerchem./1655* (initials in monogram; the signature is obscure and perhaps partly overpainted by the artist). Purchased by George IV with the Baring collection (6) in 1814 and placed in the Bow Room on the ground floor at Carlton House; formerly in the De Dufresne and De Bruyn collections, Amsterdam (H. de Groot, No.494).

The date has sometimes been read in the past as *1652,* but *1655* seems the correct reading; a drawing by Berchem of 1656 is, moreover, clearly related to this design (*Nederlandse 17e Eeuwse Italianiserende Landschapschilders,* Centraal Museum, Utrecht, 1965 (77)).

Jan Wijnants (*active by 1643; died 1684*)

45 Landscape with a Hawking Party *Plate 56*

Oil on panel: 17⅞ × 21⅞ in. Signed: *JWijnants.* Bought by George IV at the Walsh Porter sale at Christie's, 14 April 1810 (18), and placed in the room next to the Dining-Room at Carlton House; formerly in the D'Acquet and Van Leyden collections (H. de Groot, No.90).

Probably painted *c.*1665. The figures and animals in the foreground were probably painted for Wijnants by another artist; they are in the style of Lingelbach or Adriaen van de Velde, but at the time of the purchase of the picture they were attributed to Wouwermans.

Adriaen van de Velde (1636–72)

46 The Coast near Scheveningen *Plate 24*
Oil on canvas: 15⅛ × 19⅝ in. (stretched in lining). Signed and dated: *A.V.Velde.f./1660*. Purchased by George IV with the Baring collection (56) in 1814 and placed in the room next to the Dining-Room at Carlton House; formerly in the collection of the Countess of Holderness (H. de Groot, No.357).

Karel Du Jardin (1621/22(?)–1678)

47 Two Cows with a Shepherd Boy cutting a Twig *Plate 62*
Oil on panel: 14 × 12½ in. Signed: *K.DV.IARDIN* (the N is reversed). Purchased by George IV with the Baring collection (73) in 1814 and placed in the room next to the Dining-Room at Carlton House; formerly in the Choiseul and Robit collections (H. de Groot, No.69).
Probably painted *c.* 1662.

Godfried Schalcken (1643–1706)

48 Seven Persons playing a Game *Plate 32*
Oil on panel: 25¼ × 19½ in. There are traces of a signature which was formerly read as: *G. Schalcken me fecit*. Bought by H. Phillips for George IV at the Walsh Porter sale at Christie's, 23 March 1803 (47); later in the Dining-Room at Carlton House; formerly in the Van Schuylenburg collection in The Hague and in the possession of Louis XVI of France (H. de Groot, No.166).

Probably painted in Dordrecht *c.*1675–80. Houbraken, who knew the picture when it was in the Van Schuylenburg collection, described the game as *Vroutje kom ten Hoof* ('Lady, come into the Garden'), which young people used to play at parties at that period in Dordrecht. Schalcken himself appears, wearing only shirt and breeches and in the lap of a young woman in the foreground. The other figures are also presumably portraits of Schalcken's friends or members of his family (*Groote Schouburgh*, vol. III (Amsterdam, 1721), p.138; p.354 of Wurzbach's edition of 1880).

Jan Steen (1625 or 1626–1678)

49 A Twelfth Night Feast: 'The King Drinks' *Plate 46*
Oil on panel: 15⅞ × 21½ in. Signed: *IS*. Purchased by George IV with the Baring collection (18) in 1814 and placed (appropriately) in the Dining-Room at Carlton House (H. de Groot, No.498).

Painted c.1665. The scene records the moment during a Twelfth Night festivity when the 'king' drains his glass to the universal cry of: 'the king drinks'. The bellows under his left foot are probably intended to add to the noise made by the party and are in addition, a well-worn allusion to the devil; in the same way the three candles set up on the floor, shielded(?) by the little girl, symbolize the Three Kings and probably contain an allusion to pagan customs. The artist himself is seen on the other side of the table, flourishing three pipes. Above the 'king's' head is stuck a print of an owl and a monkey. In a slightly confused, and perhaps partly painted out, passage in the background, the *Starreman* and his friends are singing carols (*Jan Steen*, Mauritshuis, 1958–9 (39)).

Jan van der Heyden (1637–1712)

50 A Country House by a Canal near Delft *Plate 30*
Oil on panel: 18 $\frac{7}{16}$ × 23 $\frac{3}{16}$ in. Signed: *Heyde*. Purchased by George IV with the Baring collection (2) in 1814 and placed in the Little Blue Room at Carlton House; formerly in the collections of the Comte de Vence and Blondel de Gagny.

Probably painted c.1660: the figures may have been inserted by Adriaen van de Velde. The house has been identified as Pasgeld on the Vliet near Delft, a house demolished c.1892: '*Huis Pasgeld, aan de Haagsche Vaart*' (J. W. Niemeijer, 'De Identificatie van het Landhuis op Jan van der Heyden's Vaartgezicht ...', *Oud-Holland*, vol. LXXV (1960), pp.119–21).

Frans Post (c.1612–1680)

51 View of a Village in Brazil *Plate 53*
Oil on panel: 20$\frac{1}{8}$ × 23$\frac{1}{4}$ in. Bought with the collection of Giovanni Antonio Pellegrini by Consul Smith. No.47 of the Dutch and Flemish section of Smith's collection, sold to George III in 1762, was 'An Indian Market with many figures, board' (R. C. Smith, 'The Brazilian Landscapes of Frans Post', *Art Quarterly*, vol. I (1938), p.265; J. de Sousa-Leão, 'Frans Post in Brazil', *Burlington Magazine*, vol. LXXX (1942), p.61; E. Larsen, *Frans Post* (Amsterdam, Rio de Janeiro, 1962), p.196, No.71).

Jan van der Heyden (1637–1712)

52 The Approach to the Town of Veere *Plate 67*
Oil on panel: 18 × 22 in. Signed: *I.V.Heyde*. Probably the 'View of a Town &c' by 'A.V. & Vanderheyde' which George IV bought from William Harris on 7 February 1811 (Windsor, Royal Archives, Geo. 27087); later in the Little Blue Room at Carlton House (H. de Groot, No.109).

Probably painted *c*.1665; the figures, in contrast to those in No.50, should perhaps be attributed to Van der Heyden himself. Veere in Zeeland, on the strait between Walcheren and Noord Beveland, was formerly an important port which carried on an extensive trade with Scotland. The *Grote Kerk* was badly damaged by fire in 1686. English and French troops were quartered in it during the Napoleonic wars.

Aelbert Cuyp (1620–91)

53 Two Horsemen talking to a Peasant in a Landscape *Plate 55*
Oil on panel: 14¾ × 18½ in. Signed: *A. cüyp*. Purchased by George IV with the Baring collection (62) in 1814; recorded in the room next to the Dining-Room at Carlton House in 1816 (84). Probably painted *c*.1650 (H. de Groot, No.488). The nearer of the two horses is used by Cuyp again in his large *Negro Page,* also in the royal collection.

Adriaen van Ostade (1610–85)

54 Dutch Courtship: an Elderly Couple in an Arbour *Plate 44*
Oil on panel: 9⅛ × 7⅝ in. Signed: *Av. Ostade* (the *Av.* in monogram). Purchased by George IV with the Baring collection (86) in 1814 and placed in the room next to the Dining-Room at Carlton House (H. de Groot, No.315).

Gerrit Dou (1613–75)

55 A Couple by Candle-light *Plate 39*
Oil on panel: 10 × 7½ in. Acquired by James II and recorded in the King's Closet at Windsor during his reign (Sir L. Cust in *Burlington Magazine*, vol. XXX (1917), p.154). A copy is in the set at Welbeck of copies in miniature by Nicholas Dixon after the works of various masters (R. W. Goulding, *Catalogue of the Pictures ... at Welbeck Abbey ...* (1936), pp.439–40).

56 A Girl chopping Onions: 'Le Hachis d'Oignons' *Plate 40*

Oil on panel: $7\frac{1}{4} \times 5\frac{7}{8}$ in. Signed and dated: *GDOV* (initials in monogram) *1646*. Purchased by George IV with the Baring collection (10) in 1814 and placed in the room next to the Dining-Room at Carlton House. Formerly in the De Verrue, Gaignat, Choiseul, Conti and Choiseul-Praslin collections in Paris; later in the Trumbull and Bryan sales and in the Gildemeester collection in Amsterdam (H. de Groot, No.121; W. Martin, *Gerard Dou, Klassiker der Kunst* (Stuttgart, Berlin, 1913), 122; C. J. de Bruyn Kops, 'De Amsterdamse Verzamelaar Jan Gildemeester Jansz.', *Bulletin van het Rijksmuseum* (1965), pp.110–11; Rosenberg, Slive, Ter Kuile, pp.87–8). Enlargements made to the panel include, on the left, an area on which the design was extended by an overpainted window. In 1971 the surface was restored and the overpainting removed.

57 The Grocer's Shop *Plate 41*

Oil on panel: $19\frac{3}{16} \times 13\frac{15}{16}$ in. Signed: *GDOV./1672* (initials in monogram) and signed again on a box in the background. Bought by George IV for one thousand guineas from Thomas Thompson Martin on 21 June 1817; recorded in the Bow Room on the state floor at Carlton House. Formerly in the Choiseul-Praslin collection (H. de Groot, No.187; W. Martin, *Gerard Dou, Klassiker der Kunst* (Stuttgart, Berlin, 1913), 261).

Gabriel Metsu (1629–67)

58 Portrait of the Artist *Plate 42*

Oil on panel: $14\frac{7}{8} \times 12\frac{5}{16}$ in. Signed: *G. Metsu*. Purchased by George IV with the Baring collection (79) in 1814 and placed in the room next to the Dining-Room at Carlton House; formerly in the Pancras and Hasselaar collections in Amsterdam (H. de Groot, No.208).

Probably painted *c.*1665. The painter seems to be making in chalk a preparatory drawing for a painting on a panel. The picture gives a valuable indication of a painter's equipment at this date. The little bust of a girl, and Lucas Vorsterman's print after a *Christ at the Column* by Gerard Seghers, reappear in Metsu's picture in the National Gallery (5225) of a young girl drawing. They emphasize the value attached to drawing after sculpture and prints in the training of an artist.

Karel Du Jardin (1621/22(?)–1678)

59 A Shepherd Boy asleep with a Cow and a Calf *Plate 29*
Oil on panel: 10¾×13¾ in. Signed: *K.DV JARDIN* (the *N* is reversed).
Purchased by George IV with the Baring collection (14) and placed in
the Bow Room on the ground floor at Carlton House (H. de Groot,
No.68). Probably painted *c.*1660.

Nicholaes Berchem (1620–83)

60 A Shepherdess crossing a Stream with her Flocks *Plate 63*
Oil on copper: 13⅜ × 16 in. Signed and dated: *Berchem. 1658.* Purchased
by George IV with the Baring collection in 1814 (64) and placed in
the Bow Room on the ground floor at Carlton House (H. de Groot,
No.379). The shepherd riding on the back of the horse on the other
side of the stream had been painted out by a later hand but was restored in 1971.

Hendrick Gerritsz. Pot (c.1585–1657)

61 Charles I, Henrietta Maria and Charles, Prince of Wales *Plate 3*
Oil on panel: 18⅝ × 23½ in. Purchased by George IV, as by A. Mytens,
with the Baring collection (61) in 1814; it had been acquired by Sir
Francis Baring from the collection of Greffier Fagel in 1801. It was
in the Little Blue Room at Carlton House in 1816 (58).

The painter was in London in 1632. His portrait of Charles I in
the Louvre, signed and dated 1632, is very close to the figure of the
King in this group, but the treatment of the King's head in the two
portraits shows considerable differences in features and in the dressing
of the hair. The infant seated on the table, supported by the Queen, is
probably the Prince of Wales, the future Charles II. He had, however,
been born on 29 May 1630 and Princess Mary, the King's second child,
had been born on 4 November 1631. The child and his mother hold
sprigs of olive, in allusion to the peace-loving nature of the King's
father, James I; leaves of laurel, scattered on the floor, refer to the
martial career of the Queen's father, Henri IV of France. Van Dyck
made use slightly later of the olive and the laurel to point to the union
of peace and war in the marriage of Charles I and Henrietta Maria and
in their issue; in his masque, *Love's Wel-come . . . at Bolsover* (1634), Ben
Jonson struck the same note (O. Millar, 'Some Painters and Charles I',
Burlington Magazine, vol. CIV (1962), p.329). The regalia in Pot's two
English royal portraits bears no resemblance to the regalia in portraits
of the King by Mytens or Van Dyck. Houbraken records in his *Groote*

Schouburgh (vol. II, 1719, p.97; p.214 of Wurzbach's edition of 1880) that Pot had painted 'den Brittanischen Koning met zyne gemalin naar 't leven, nevens verscheiden grooten van dat Ryk'.

Adriaen van de Velde (1636–72)

62 Cattle, Sheep and a Donkey resting under Trees with a sleeping Shepherdess *Plate 61*
Oil on panel: $14\frac{7}{8} \times 16\frac{7}{8}$ in. Signed and dated: *A.V.Velde. f. 1668*. Purchased by George IV with the Baring collection (81) in 1814 and placed in the Dining-Room at Carlton House; formerly in the collection of the Countess of Holderness (H. de Groot, Nos.210, 261).

Adriaen van Ostade (1610–85)

63 Peasants in a Tavern *Plate 43*
Oil on panel: $14\frac{1}{2} \times 12\frac{3}{4}$ in. Signed and dated: *Av. Ostade, 1665* (the *Av.* in monogram); the signature is on a label which bears a notice, in Dutch, that this house is for sale: enquire from the painter. Purchased by George IV with the Baring collection (78) in 1814 and placed in the Bow Room on the ground floor at Carlton House; formerly in the Van Slingeland collection in Dordrecht (H. de Groot, No.645).

Gerard Ter Borch (1617–81)

64 A Couple seated over a Glass of Wine *Plate 48*
Oil on canvas (formerly mounted on a panel which was removed, 1961/2): $16\frac{1}{2} \times 12\frac{1}{2}$ in. Purchased for George IV in 1812 and placed in the Prince Regent's Ante-Room at Carlton House; formerly in the Peilhon and Abbé Leblanc collections.

Painted *c.*1660. S. J. Gudlaugsson recognizes in the woman the features of Ter Borch's step-sister Gesina (1631–90); a costume very like hers is seen again in No.26. The carpet and table are also used elsewhere by Ter Borch (*Gerard Ter Borch* (The Hague), vol. I (1959), pp.131–2, pl.166; vol. II (1960), p.170 (No.166)).

Jan Weenix (1642(?)–1719)

65 A Dead Hare with Dead Birds and Implements of the Chase *Plate 73*
Oil on canvas: $43\frac{3}{4} \times 36$ in. Signed and dated: *J.Weenix. A* [or *f*] *1704*. Purchased by George IV with the Baring collection (22).

Hendrick Avercamp (1585–1634)

De Stomme van Kampen – the Mute of Kampen – Avercamp spent almost all his life in his native town and his ice-bound landscapes in oil and his watercolour drawings record the winter scenery and pastimes on the river Ijsel at the point where it flows into the Zuider Zee. The drawings in this exhibition are all in pencil or red chalk, with pen and ink and washes of colour. The more fanciful attempts by C. J. Welcker and L. van Puyvelde to identify the people in the drawings have not been repeated. The most recent discussion of a number of the Avercamps in the royal collection is in the catalogue, *Masterpieces of the Dutch School from the Collection of H.M. the King of England*, Mauritshuis, 1948 (11–29).

66 A Young Man skating
$6\frac{3}{4} \times 4\frac{1}{2}$ in. (Welcker, T.147; Puyvelde, No.26).

67 A Young Couple on the Ice
$5\frac{5}{8} \times 5\frac{1}{8}$ in. (Welcker, T.154; Puyvelde, No.33). The figure of the girl has been cut out and pasted on to the sheet beside her companion.

68 A Fashionable Party, in a Horse-drawn Sleigh
$5\frac{1}{2} \times 7\frac{3}{4}$ in. (Welcker, T.139; Puyvelde, No.18).

69 Figures on the Ice; a Young Man playing Golf
$7 \times 9\frac{3}{8}$ in. (Welcker, T.140; Puyvelde, No.19).

70 The Knife-Grinder
$6\frac{1}{2} \times 7\frac{7}{8}$ in. (Welcker, T.141; Puyvelde, No.20).

71 A Fashionable Party on the Ice
$8\frac{1}{4} \times 12\frac{3}{4}$ in. (Welcker, T.135; Puyvelde, No.15).

72 A Couple on Horseback
$4\frac{7}{8} \times 3\frac{3}{8}$ in. (Welcker, T.151; Puyvelde, No.30).

73 A Hay-Waggon on a Ferry
$3\frac{1}{8} \times 6\frac{1}{4}$ in. (Welcker, T.173; Puyvelde, No.52).

74 A Young Lady with a Muff
$5\frac{1}{8} \times 2\frac{5}{8}$ in. (Welcker, T.165; Puyvelde, No.43).

75 A Young Lady seen from behind
$5\frac{7}{8} \times 2\frac{5}{8}$ in. (Welcker, T.163; Puyvelde, No.42).

76 View of Kampen
$4\frac{1}{8} \times 12\frac{1}{4}$ in. Signed: *HA* (in monogram). (Welcker, T.177; Puyvelde, No.56).

77 **Fishermen with a Sleigh**
$3\frac{3}{4} \times 4\frac{1}{4}$ in. (Welcker, T.169; Puyvelde, No.48).

78 **A Horse-drawn Sleigh going through the Ice**
$3\frac{5}{8} \times 7\frac{3}{8}$ in. (Welcker, T.171; Puyvelde, No.50).

79 **Figures on the Ice; a Fashionable Party grouped round a Horse-drawn Sleigh**
$6\frac{7}{8} \times 11\frac{1}{2}$ in. (Welcker, T.136; Puyvelde, No.16).

80 **Figures on the Ice**
$7\frac{1}{4} \times 7\frac{7}{8}$ in. (Welcker, T.142; Puyvelde, No.21).

81 **A Fisherman and a Milkmaid by a Canal**
$5\frac{1}{8} \times 7\frac{5}{8}$ in. (Welcker, T.144; Puyvelde, No.23).

82 **A *Boejer* (?)**
$8 \times 6\frac{1}{8}$ in. (Welcker, T.182; Puyvelde, No.62).

83 **Two Young Men**
$4\frac{1}{16} \times 5\frac{7}{8}$ in. (Welcker, T.148; Puyvelde, No.27).

84 **An Elderly Couple on the Ice**
$4\frac{1}{2} \times 5\frac{1}{4}$ in. (Welcker, T.150; Puyvelde, No.29).

Godfried Schalcken (1643–1706)

85 **The Concert** *Plate 75*
Oil on panel: $22\frac{3}{4} \times 18\frac{3}{4}$ in. Signed: *G. Schalcken./fecit*. Possibly to be identified with 'A Painting an Interior – by – Godfrey Schalcken' which seems to have been acquired by George IV through Lord Yarmouth in November 1810; by 1816 it was certainly in the Dining-Room at Carlton House; formerly in the Grill, Hasselaer and Gildemeester collections in Amsterdam (H. de Groot, No.160).

Probably painted *c.*1665–70. The young man standing in the background is almost certainly a self-portrait. Doubts have been expressed recently as to the authenticity of the picture, on the grounds of the pigment used in it; but these doubts are not easy to reconcile with what is known of the picture's history.

Adam Willaerts (1577–1664)

86 **The Embarkation of a Prince** *Plate 4*
Oil on canvas: $48 \times 77\frac{1}{2}$ in. Signed and dated: *A Willarts. fe 1623*. Purchased by Queen Victoria in 1858.

The subject has not been identified with certainty. The date, and the badge of the Prince of Wales on the barge at the landing-stage, led in the past to the belief that the scene was the review of the fleet by James I before it set sail to escort the Prince of Wales (the future Charles I) back to England from Spain. The figures in the foreground and their actions, which indicate a formal leave-taking by a young Prince and Princess, do not support this suggestion. The picture is very closely related to a picture by Willaerts, signed and dated 1622, in the National Maritime Museum. The two pictures almost certainly record the embarkation at Margate on 25 April 1613 of the newly married Princess Elizabeth and the Elector Palatine. A third painting, signed and dated 1623 and in the Craven collection, shows the couple arriving at Flushing four days later.

The Standard flown in the *Prince Royal* (built in 1610 by Phineas Pett under the auspices of Henry, Prince of Wales) was used by the Earl of Nottingham, commander of the squadron; under the bows can be seen the *Distain*, a miniature ship made for the Prince by Pett in 1604 so that he could amuse himself on the Thames near London Bridge.

Adriaen van der Werff (1659–1722)

87 Two Children with a Kitten and a Guinea-Pig *Plate 47*
Oil on canvas: 12⅞ × 10¾ in. Signed and dated: *A VD WERF Fec.ᵗ 1681* (the *VD* in monogram). Purchased by George IV with the Baring collection (58) in 1814 and placed in the Bow Room on the state floor at Carlton House; formerly in the Nijman collection in Amsterdam (H. de Groot, No.168).

Willem van Mieris (1662–1747)

88 The Neglected Guitar *Plate 49*
Oil on panel: 18½ × 15¼ in. Purchased by George IV with the Baring collection (63) in 1814 and placed in the Ante-Room on the ground floor at Carlton House; formerly in the De Vogel collection in Amsterdam (H. de Groot, No.290).

On grounds of costume, No.88 could probably be dated *c.*1695. There are obvious allusions to the pleasures of taste (in the oysters and wine) leading to the pleasures of love, after the couple have enjoyed the pleasures of music.

89 The Fruiterer's Shop *Plate 50*
Oil on panel: 15 3/16 × 12½ in. Signed and dated: *W. van Mieris, Feᵗ Anᵒ 1732*. Probably to be identified with 'a Beautiful Cabinet Picture by Mieris' which George IV bought from Philip Hill on 14 May 1805

94

(Windsor, Royal Archives, Geo. 26826). By 1816 in the room next to the Dining-Room at Carlton House (H. de Groot, No.194).

Salomon van Ruysdael (1600/3(?)–70)

90 A River Landscape *Plate 52*
Oil on panel: 17¾ × 26⅝ in. Signed and dated: *SvR. 1651* (the *vR* in monogram). Recorded at Hampton Court early in the reign of Queen Victoria (W. Stechow, *Salomon van Ruysdael* (Berlin, 1938), p.101, No. 289).

Cornelis Saftleven (1607–81)

91 Two Pigs awaiting Slaughter *Plate 69*
Oil on panel: 6¼ × 9⅛ in.; the panel had been enlarged at a later date on all sides making it 9½ × 12 in., and these additions were removed in 1970. Signed with the painter's monogram (*CSL?*) and dated *1657*. The additions bore a later, false, Potter signature; Saftleven's monogram has been noticed recently, e.g., by Mr Christopher White. Purchased by George IV with the Baring collection (66) in 1814 and placed in the Bow Room on the state floor at Carlton House; formerly in the Slingelandt collection in Dort (H. de Groot, as Potter, No.129). A drawing in Rotterdam of a pig, dated 1644 and closely related to No.91, is now attributed to Saftleven, having been formerly attributed to Potter.

Willem van Aelst (1627–83)

92 Dead Birds with Implements of the Chase *Plate 72*
Oil on canvas: 41½ × 35½ in. Signed and dated: *W.V.aelst.1657*. Almost certainly in the collection of Charles II; recorded in the reign of James II, hanging in the King's Closet in the Private Lodgings at Whitehall.

Michiel van Miereveld (1567–1641)

93 An Old Man holding a Shell *Plate 36*
Oil on panel: 34½ × 26½ in. In the collection of Prince Henry, whose brand (HP) is on the back with a label, applied under the eye of Abraham van der Doort, stating that the picture was among those which had passed to Charles I on the death of his elder brother. Since the Restoration it has been confusingly described successively as a self-portrait and as a portrait of Cornelius or Thomas Johnson.

Maerten van Heemskerck (1498–1574)

94 Jonah under the Gourd *Plate 33*

Oil on panel: $16\frac{1}{8} \times 31\frac{1}{8}$ in. Signed and dated: *Aᵒ 1561/Martynus Van/ Heemskerck/Inventor*. Purchased by Charles II from William Frizell in 1660 and placed in the King's Privy Gallery at Whitehall. The picture illustrates Jonah IV.6: Jonah seated in the shade of the gourd on the east side of Nineveh.

33 *Maerten van Heemskerck* (No.94)

34 *Hendrick Gerritsz. Pot* (No.2)

35 *Adriaen Hanneman* (No.3)

36 *Michiel van Miereveld* (No.93)

37 *Rembrandt* (No.7)

38 *Daniel Mytens* (No.6)

39 *Gerrit Dou* (No.55)

40 *Gerrit Dou* (No.56)

41 *Gerrit Dou* (No.57)

42 *Gabriel Metsu* (No.58)

43 *Adriaen van Ostade* (No.63)

44 *Adriaen van Ostade* (No.54)

46 *Jan Steen* (No.49)

45 *Jan Steen* (No.20)

47 *Adriaen van der Werff* (No.87)

48 *Gerard Ter Borch* (No.64)

49 *Willem van Mieris* (No.88)

50 *Willem van Mieris* (No.89)

51 *Paulus Potter* (No.34)

52 *Salomon van Ruysdael* (No.90)

53 *Frans Post* (No.51)

54 *Meyndert Hobbema* (No.24)

55 *Aelbert Cuyp* (No.53)

56 *Jan Wijnants* (No.45)

58 *Philips Wouwermans* (No.31)

57 *Philips Wouwermans* (No.39)

59 *Adriaen van de Velde* (No.32)

60 *Adriaen van de Velde* (No.36)

61 *Adriaen van de Velde* (No.62)

62 *Karel Du Jardin* (No.47)

63 *Nicolaes Berchem* (No.60)

64 *Nicolaes Berchem* (No.28)

65 *Willem van de Velde the Younger* (No.18)

66 *Willem van de Velde the Younger* (No.23)

67 *Jan van der Heyden* (No.52)

68 *Willem van de Velde the Younger* (No.41)

69 *Cornelis Saftleven* (No.91)

70 *Adriaen Hanneman* (No.8)

71 *Sir Peter Lely* (No.16)

72 *Willem van Aelst* (No.92)

73 *Jan Weenix* (No.65)

74 *Melchior de Hondecoeter* (No.30)

75 *Godfried Schalcken* (No.85)